FRANTZ PROSCHOWSKY

THE WAY TO SING

A GUIDE TO VOCALISM
WITH THIRTY PRACTICAL EXERCISES

By
FRANTZ PROSCHOWSKY
ILLUSTRATED BY THE AUTHOR

PRICE $2.25

BOSTON
C. C. BIRCHARD & COMPANY

COPYRIGHT, MCMXXIII
BY
C. C. BIRCHARD & COMPANY
COPYRIGHT RENEWED AND ASSIGNED
TO
C. C. BIRCHARD & COMPANY
International Copyright Secured

Printed in U. S. A.

2–52

To
MADAME GALLI-CURCI
THE WORLD'S GREATEST SINGER

AUTHOR'S PREFACE

About ten years ago, while conducting classes for teachers and advanced students, I began the practice of answering and analyzing intelligently prepared questions relating to the Art of Singing. Practically these answers were brief lectures on the topics so introduced, and they form the basis of this book.

I believe in no method that does not closely follow Nature's intention. I believe in no lost or refound Art of Singing. Neither do I believe that voices can be made. The Voice, as we use the term here, is a gift. The manufactured Voice does not exist, despite the claims of the "voice-creators."

The main principles laid down in this work are based on indisputable facts. I have tried to illustrate the truth of *Cause* and *Effect* in the various phases of voice production and vocalization. My whole thesis is opposition to everything *unnatural* in the study and practice of the Art. Nature alone has provided the true *Method* of singing. It remains for us to apply it.

The exercises are based on my own experience with pupils of many nationalities whose characteristics I have carefully studied; and in this connection I will say that my frequent warnings against the wrong use of the nasal quality are addressed chiefly to the English speaking race. If, anywhere in the book, I have seemed to repeat myself, it has been done deliberately with the purpose of impressing on my readers the importance of the principles involved.

I trust that the following pages will reveal and clarify some of the principles of the Art of Singing which are so often hidden in vague and obscure generalities.

FRANTZ PROSCHOWSKY

CONTENTS

	PAGE
PURPOSE	1
CHAPTER I	2
Talent	2
Methods	3
CHAPTER II	6
Acoustics	6
CHAPTER III	11
Vocal Organs	11
Tongue Bone	14
Windpipe	15
False Vocal Chords	16
Tonsils	17
Uvula	17
CHAPTER IV	19
Production of the Voice	19
Voice Classification	20
Technique	20
Sense of Touch	22
CHAPTER V	24
Vocal Chord Mechanism	24
Register and Registers	24
Attack	31
CHAPTER VI	33
Abnormal Breathing	33
Normal Breathing	35
Breath Form — Tone Color	40
Support	44
Review on Breathing	45
CHAPTER VII	47
Pianissimo and Forte	47
Crescendo and Diminuendo	47
CHAPTER VIII	50
Nasal Support	50
Larynx, Palate, Tongue and Mouth	51
CHAPTER IX	53
Vowels and Consonants	53
Consonants	59
The Vowel E	60
CHAPTER X	65
Articulation	65
Normal Voice	66
Low Medium, C to G	68
Intonation	69

CONTENTS

	PAGE
Throaty or Guttural	74
Covering	75
Open Singing	77
Somber Timbre	78
Bright Timbre	79
Singing Forward	79
Diffused Singing	80
Humming	81
Head Voice	82
Vibrating Air-Column	84
Tenor-Barytone	85
Laryngoscope Observations	87
CHAPTER XI	89
Study of Text	89
Poise	92
Concentration	93
General Review	94
CHAPTER XII	97
The Low Larynx	97
CHAPTER XIII	99
The Trill	99
As a Remedy for Tremolo	100
Staccato	100
Bad Methods	102
CHAPTER XIV	103
Song and Songs	103
Mental Side of Singing	104
Balance	106
CHAPTER XV	107
Hygiene of the Voice	107
Colds	107
The Throat	107
Causes of Trouble	108
Fear	108
The Teacher's Function	109
Hoarseness	109
General Advice	110
CHAPTER XVI	111
Suggestions in Plastic	111
Concert Singers	111
Opera	112
CHAPTER XVII	114
Tables of Poise and Gesture	114
EXERCISES	117–131

The Way to Sing

Purpose

So many works on the Art of Singing treat the subject more from the standpoint of fancy than fact, that it is difficult for the serious student to find logical explanations for the many obstacles which usually present themselves during the progress of study. It is my purpose to explain the Art of Singing in *Cause and Effect*, from a *mental* as well as a physical viewpoint, thus giving student, artist and teacher a definite key to the solving of the various problems to be encountered during the period of first studies, as well as during further development. To learn to sing means to learn to hear. The keener the ear is trained to recognize perfect, less perfect and imperfect tone-production, the nearer is the singer himself to perfection. The ear mentally guides and should stand supreme in making the physical organs obey and produce the desired results; this, naturally, within the limits of each individual's ability. A singer thus trained to recognize, through hearing, the causes which produce the effects desired, stands safe in building a career reaching to the full limitations of his talent and natural vocal endowments. This definite knowledge lacking, growth is limited and the technique not to be relied upon. Therefore we want facts and not fancies, and it is my purpose to enable my readers to see deeper into the mental and physical conditions which control the causes of the desired effects, thus converting abstract knowledge into concrete knowledge and upon this solid foundation develop individuality.

CHAPTER I

Talent

Besides a good natural voice, many other qualities are necessary for success; and before giving any advice, the teacher should exercise great care in estimating such qualities. A natural talent for music, effective physical appearance, artistic temperament and a sense of drama are valuable assets. Health, intelligence, common sense and the courage to hear the truth, however unflattering, are indispensable to the best results.

At the outset the teacher usually has to allow for an over-estimate of the pupil's natural qualifications. Self-criticism is not often met with in young students, who are almost invariably misled by admiring friends and relations; and therein lies the opportunity of unscrupulous teachers to flatter and promise great things — promises not often fulfilled, otherwise Melbas and Carusos would be the rule rather than the exception. Diligence and perseverance are great factors, but these can never supply shortcomings which nature may have ungraciously imposed. Unexpected and wonderful results sometimes happen in the course of a pupil's training — but rarely. My experience has enabled me clearly to define a student's capabilities in a few months of study.

For the sincere as well as wise teacher will tell his pupil the whole truth, and, with the advantage of a clean, honest start, will frequently produce a singer of merit from what was not the most promising material.

An early beginning of vocal study is urged, before material cares arise to distract the mind. Of all the arts, none is more dependent on an early beginning and singleness of purpose. Even vocal prodigies have not been exempt from incessant industry in maintaining their high standards of art.

We find talents of various kinds: rare vocal phenomena; voices of less beauty but accompanied by great dramatic and temperamental gifts; voices coupled with extraordinary musical equipment. All of these qualities are seldom found together, but when they are, we have *genius*. However, I have also seen cases where all of the above mentioned qualifications were present and yet valueless for want of earnest application. So let it be said that without application and hard work one can never develop natural gifts, however great. He may become an amateur singer, pleasing to himself and his friendly audience; and we do not under-rate that result, which is often the best and most satisfactory issue of the matter.

Let the student develop his capacity for self-criticism, and learn to discount flattery and irresponsible advice. It is not possible for all students to reach the highest attainments; genius alone does that; but, given a fair allotment of the essential qualities herein described, the earnest student can and does achieve the most gratifying success.

Methods

Any method giving good results is a good method; the name of the method matters but little, — what we want is results. The method so often spoken of as the Italian method is frequently misunderstood, — as are the so-called French and German methods. The Italians have vocal methods, better called vocal exercises, the growth of many years, and they also have up to the present time produced the world's greatest singers. I, however, hold this to be due chiefly to their beautiful pure vowel language; which naturally trains the Italian ear to a keener hearing regarding purity of tone — unimpaired by such disadvantages as the gutteral sounds of the German language and the overnasal tones of the French language, not to speak of our English tongue which we abuse to an abominable degree. We often hear our own singers complain of their native tongue as a medium of vocal expression. They are convinced that they sing better in French, Italian or German, overlooking the fact that, if they would give the matter of *diction* in their own language the same amount of study they devote to it in other languages, the result would be amazing. Every language can be sung perfectly by a singer of any nationality if the true knowledge of the art of singing is based on the fundamental practise of the Italians, to specify the nation that has produced the greatest singers.

Much literature exists on the point of the differences of method. I believe that Manuel Garcia in his " Art of Singing " and " Hints on Singing " has given the students as healthy and safe advice and exercises as can be found. Marchesi, Viardot, Garcia, Gerster and several others have also written so-called methods, but in reality they are inferior imitations of Manuel Garcia's works. Gerster went to the extreme of marking differences in registers in different colors of print, — a most dangerous and confusing conception of the art of singing.

Madame Lehmann's book on singing is to be taken only as her own conception and personal understanding of the art, a book that she regrets having written and for which she defends herself in later years. As a practical work it could not be recommended, as it is illogical; and yet valuable suggestions are to be found in it for those who are far enough advanced to exercise discrimination. As for Lilli Lehmann herself, she is a Queen of Song. I heard her sing magnificently at the age of seventy-one. Her high C could justly have been envied by any young singer.

Then there are the vast numbers of methods and treatises on singing, — most of them contravening other methods. Some of these methods are all mental, others all physical or all scientific, — each striving to make clear — something. However, in most works on singing there is, here and there, some good advice; but whether it pays to read them all for what little good may be derived from them, is a question. I must warn the readers of the general literature on singing to be careful of vague statements that have no logical explanation. Much confusing literature exists on this subject.

The German work on "Singing and Speaking" by Hay, is of some value; but it was written primarily for Germans and especially for the use of Wagnerian singers. I have heard many exponents of the Hay exercises of vocal diction. The theoretical side of the work is carried out in detail, but it is not practical. If the underlying principles of the pure art were more clearly emphasized than are the German difficulties, the amount of energy spent on this work would mean something. It is, at best, only for Germans with German voices and for Wagnerian music in German.

Theory and practice must go hand in hand. A teacher of any method must be able to demonstrate his art in sound, healthy tone-production and in artistic and musical phrasing, or he is not qualified to teach the art of singing. He must possess knowledge, patience and judgment,— must, in short, be servant and master in one.

CHAPTER II

Acoustics

The phenomena of acoustics and its underlying principles are best described by comparative illustrations.

Sound is a vibration of molecules or atoms and is transmitted through the air by one molecule impinging upon another, and setting up in it a similar vibration. Any object placed in the path of these vibrating atoms is set into motion or vibration in exact proportion to the atoms with which it comes into contact. The tympanum, or eardrum, is an object in the path of sound and consequently responds, as does any inanimate membrane, to perpendicular motion. Our sense of hearing is nothing more than a transmission by the nerve connecting the eardrum and the brain of a state of unrest or non-equilibrium of the former mentioned vibrations. It is important to note that sound is not a movement of a body of air from place to place but a vibration of the particles of air which, as soon as the disturbance ceases, return to a state of rest.

We are all familiar with the example of the man hewing wood,— we see the impact of the axe on the log and after a short space of time we hear the concussion of the blow. The explanation is that it has taken the sound some time to transverse the distance between the hewer and the observer.

An optical illustration as to how waves travel is usually demonstrated by dropping a stone into a placid body of water. One notices around the center of disturbance a number of ever-increasing concentric circles. If you now place upon this surface of water a small float, you will notice that this float will assume a to-and-fro movement but that its relative position will remain unchanged after its lateral movement has ceased. Transform in your imagination this float into a particle of infinitesimal proportions and the body of water into a body of air and then you will have the vibration caused by sound on the particles of air.

Intensity. Should these sound vibrations have a large amplitude in comparison to the length, we are impressed by a sudden powerful disturbance which is equivalent to what we call intensity or volume.

Pitch. Should these sound vibrations be very rapid, the sound or tone will be high. The greater the number of vibrations per second, the higher is the tone.

Tone Color. Should these sound vibrations be affected by enclosed space (mouth), material (wood as in a flute) and so forth, so that the vibration sets up minor vibrations in the adjacent molecules, then we have *color* which distinguishes the tone.

We have, in our illustrations, referred to lateral vibration. In reality the sound waves travel in all directions from the point of emanation and consequently fill all space. The intensity of sound diminishes in proportion to the square of the distance, *i.e.*, a bell having the intensity of one at a distance of one meter has the intensity of one-fourth or is one-fourth as strong or loud at a distance of two meters. This, however, is the case only where space is unlimited. In an enclosure such as a room, this law does not hold good because reflections of sound from the walls and ceiling alter the waves; the same is the case when talking or singing through a megaphone.

The French naturalist Biot observed that the sewers of Paris were able to transmit the softest conversation to a distance of one thousand meters.

A bare room is acoustically hard, whereas one draped

and carpeted is soft, due to the non-reflection of the walls. If sound be produced in a long narrow hall, the waves reflected from the furthermost wall interfere with the outgoing ones, producing indistinctness. Such a hall is spoken of as having "bad acoustics," meaning that it is wrongly proportioned.

The effect of vibrations depends upon their immediate surroundings and the response of the latter to the initial impulse. Imagine a string, drawn tightly between two solid bodies, to be "picked"; the emanating sound is dull. The same string placed on a violin or guitar emits an entirely different sound which is pleasing. This is called *resonance*. The body of the instrument reverberates sympathetically with the vibratory member and so gives quality and color. The same is the case with the human voice. The skull represents the body of the violin,— the vocal chords the string, and the breath the bow.

Overtones, a word often used but rarely perfectly understood, are secondary and partial vibrations which alter the shape and augment the fundamental tone wave.

Those desiring to further their knowledge of acoustics and overtones from a scientific standpoint, should read the magnificent work, "Tonemplindungen," by Helmholtz.

Every tone or sound has a dominant tone consisting of a fixed number of vibrations per second causing the various tones in our scales. The secondary vibrations do not change these fundamental and fixed number of vibrations per second but simply change the form of the vibrations,— and this is *overtone* or *color*. Pleasant tones always result when overtones are a multiple of the fundamental or basic tone,— inharmonious or harsh tones when these secondary vibrations are not synchronous.

The calculation of the major scale of all keys is as follows:

The ground tone (Tonic) C (large third) E (large fifth) G
1:                        5 4:   3 2

When we add to this the dominant G, B, D and the subdominant F, A, C, both having the Tonic C in common, we have the tones of the scale of C Major in the following proportions:

C	D	E	F	G	A	B	C
1	9/8	5/4	4/3	3/2	5/3	15/8	2

or in vibrations per second:

C	D	E	F	G	A	B	C
264	297	330	352	396	440	495	528

The lowest tone in orchestra music is E Contrabass with forty-one and one-half vibrations. Modern pianos and organs usually go to C, thirty-three vibrations. Some organs have still one octave lower with sixteen and one-half vibrations. All of these notes or tones are not in perfect intonation and are noticed only by highly musically trained perceptions. Perfect intonation is only possible on instruments having no fixed keys — such as the violin and the voice.

When we strike in succession on the piano C, E, G with the open pedal we hear many additional tones, less intensively, however. These are overtones and harmonize with the fundamental C, E, G and produce a well-balanced full acoustic satisfaction.

Striking, for instance, C, D, B successively we notice sounds unpleasant to the ear. In other words the overtones do not sympathize and the effect is disagreeable. We term these sounds discords.

An interesting experiment showing the result of tone-waves which do not coincide is the following: Two singers singing the same tone on the same vowel, at the same time, produce only one distinct tone of great volume. If, however, one sings, for example, an Italian A, the other an

Italian I, we distinguish in spite of the increased volume two distinct sounds which prove that the two vowels have distinct character and wave formation.

That intensity is proportional to the amplitude of a wave, we can prove by striking a string of a guitar. The swing or vibration of the string is readily discernable. The larger this swing or amplitude, the louder the produced tone.

These illustrations are only intended to help the mind to understand *cause* and *effect*, which is necessary for further development.

Before closing this subject we wish to repeat:

1. *Intonation* or *tone height* is directly proportional to the number of vibrations per second.

2. *Tone volume* is proportional to the amplitude of vibration, or swinging movement.

3. *Tone color* is dependent upon the different forms of the tone waves vibrating at the same time.

CHAPTER III
Vocal Organs

Definite vocal understanding is not possible without some knowledge of the vocal organs and their relative action in producing the voice. As all of our vocal organs have functions other than that of producing the singing voice, I naturally keep close to those which concern only singing. I classify vocal organs as follows: breathing apparatus, vibrating organs, articulating organs and resonators.

The drawing showing the parts of the trunk and head of the human body which have to do with tone production, is an intersection, thus showing the parts invisible to the eye in their relative positions and proportions.

The visible parts of the vocal organs are:

The **outer mouth**, (lips), having a distinct function in producing some consonants and also in aiding to a certain extent the formation of certain vowels.

The **tongue**, in a relaxed position fitting snugly the bottom of the mouth with the lower teeth as a barrier. The rear end or root of the tongue descends the throat and is also called the *base* of the tongue.

The **palate**. The roof of the mouth or hard palate extends from the upper teeth backwards to the soft palate, which terminates in the **uvula**. The part of the soft palate to the right and left of the uvula and extending from the hard palate is called the *veils* of the palate.

The invisible vocal organs are seen in the illustration on page 12.

PLATE 1

A. *Resonating*
B. *Articulating*
C. *Vibration*
D. *Reservoir*
E. *Bellows (abdomen)*
F. *Point of inhaling*
G. *Diaphragm (before inhaling)*
H.   ,,   (low ,,)

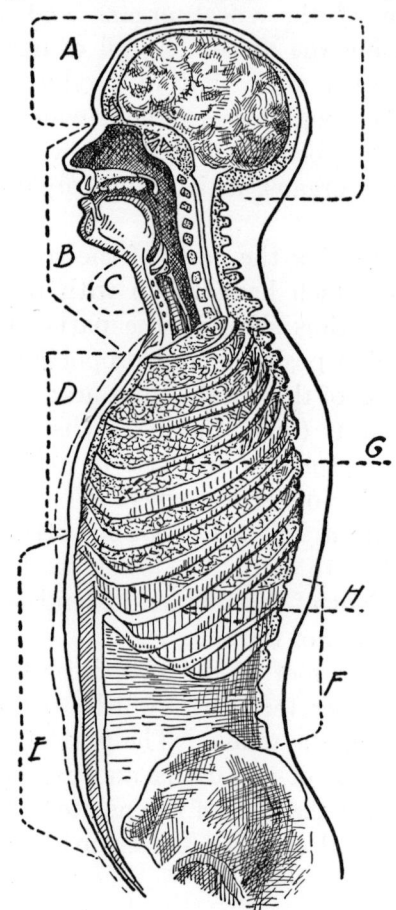

Above and in back of the palate is a large space connecting with the nasal cavity and called the **pharynx**. From here downward the throat divides into two channels, the rear for food and drink, the front for breathing and the production of sound.

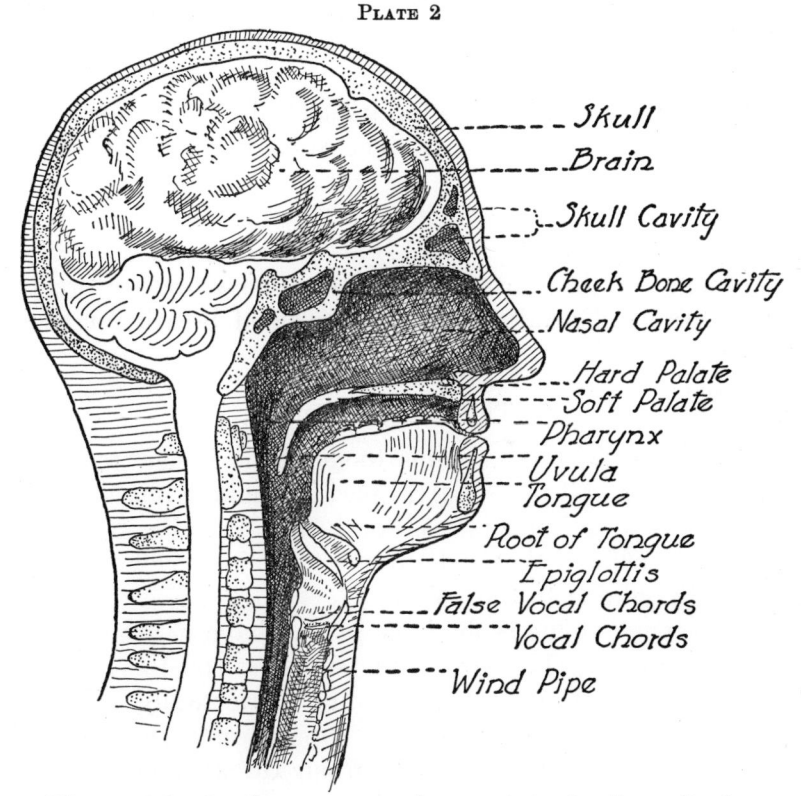

PLATE 2

Skull
Brain
Skull Cavity
Cheek Bone Cavity
Nasal Cavity
Hard Palate
Soft Palate
Pharynx
Uvula
Tongue
Root of Tongue
Epiglottis
False Vocal Chords
Vocal Chords
Wind Pipe

The **epiglottis** (larynx cover) prevents food stuffs from entering the windpipe in the process of eating. This cover or epiglottis plays a most important part in singing and will be referred to later under "Vocal Construction."

The **larynx** or "Adam's Apple" occupies a place in the throat between the root of the tongue and the upper end of the windpipe, and the vocal chords are extended horizontally from front to back within the larynx.

The lungs form the continuation and the termination of the windpipe and are separated from the digestive organs by the diaphragm which, resting on the digestive tract, is held on both sides and in the front by the abdominal walls and in the back by the spine. This digestive tract rests downward on the dorsal.

The organs described so far are actually in function while the tone is being produced. The resonating parts, at times called *reflectors*, belong to the stationary bone-structure of the head (the skull) and its resonance is dependent upon the adjustment and use of the other organs described, especially of the vibratory organs. The vibratory organs are entirely dependent upon the exhaled breath for their action.

The Tongue-Bone

Even the existence of this tongue-bone is new to many a singer — and it plays a great part in singing; but although its separate training is useless, I shall describe it briefly for the benefit of those who desire to be informed of everything pertaining to the voice.

The tongue-bone is the bone in the shape of a horseshoe or a wishbone. The two open points rest on the horns of the thyroids, the arch protruding horizontally forward. This arch of the tongue-bone is capable of expanding and when we hold our two fingers on our throat under the jaw bone, we feel the expansion when we open our throat as if swallowing. This movement of expansion also occurs during singing, keeping the throat open, and the root of the tongue sufficiently apart, to enable the epiglottis to perform with freedom while assisting in the production of vowels.

I have known vocal methods based upon the principle

of training the tongue-bone to expand, but the practice of such methods, to my knowledge, has never been successful. The tones produced became white and characterless, the voices in general too open and flattened. While I attach no value to the direct training of the tongue-bone, I fully appreciate its importance, but only as indirectly trained under the sensation of a loose, free, open throat, not an over-stretching of the so-called open throat.

The Windpipe

The windpipe plays a greater part in our singing than is usually ascribed to it. It is the downward connection between larynx and lungs and divides in the form of a T, as it directly connects with the lungs.

The windpipe is a tube constructed of cartilage rings not connecting in the back; when the cartilage ceases the tube or pipe is constructed of an elastic wall of sinewy skin that serves to separate the windpipe from the foodpipe. The windpipe, on account of this elastic wall in the back, is capable of expanding or resisting as the air used in singing is introduced, and the real compression of our breath is here adjusted, the lungs being the reservoir and the abdominal muscles gradually but automatically under normal conditions keeping the compression of air in the windpipe replenished as the flow of breath is being converted into resonance through the vibrations of the vocal chords.

In the low voice, where the vibrations are slower and heavier than in the higher voice, there is a transmission of vibration down in the upper chest where the windpipe divides into the T shape. From this sensation the term chest-voice originated, but as a resonator the chest plays no actual part.

The foregoing statements are only made for those who desire to know the part played by the windpipe in tone production, but to give that organ any further direct importance as regards training, would be out of place.

False Vocal Chords

Many errors exist in theory regarding the *false vocal chords*, also called "Lips of Morgani," — being named after their first observer, an Italian physician. The false vocal chords are placed in the larynx like loose folds forming a horizontal oblong pocket, just above the true vocal chords.

Many theories have existed regarding the purpose of the false vocal chords,— for instance: that falsetto was produced by the false vocal chords. Many other statements have been made that were more fancies than facts. One theory as to vibrations taking on modulations of form according to the opening or expanding of these pockets, still remains unproven; and as these movements can never be definitely controlled and only exist in theory, my advice is not to attach any importance to the claim.

But what is of real importance and usually not known to the singer, is that in the false vocal chords there are numerous glands that discharge moisture which flows downward into the bottom of the larynx and helps to keep the vocal chords moist. The vibrations of the true vocal chords are the means of producing this flow of moisture while singing. Those singing with breathy tone, tone where the vibrations are weak, find that this discharge of moisture ceases and this results in dry vocal chords, or husky voice. The same condition is frequently experienced by voices who substitute falsetto, or an open glottis tone, for perfect pianissimo. These voices usually find the tones immediately following the wrongly produced pianissimo to be either veiled or husky and in many cases below pitch.

In some cases the false vocal chords are diseased, in which case a reliable physician should be consulted.

Tonsils

Much has been said and written by so-called authorities *pro* and *con*, regarding the tonsils. Some recommend their removal — others write big books on their importance and warn against their removal; but all of these sayings mean little to the practical observer.

The fact remains that we have great singers who have had their tonsils removed and others who have not. Removal by incompetent physicians and the impairment of muscles and nerves of the inner throat, is of course, a detriment to the voice; but if the operation has been performed with skill and judgment, it has to my knowledge and experience never been a detriment but repeatedly a gain in health, and a usual benefit to the singers who had previously been subject to colds and unhealthy vocal organs. Good surgical advice is recommended in all cases of abnormal or unhealthy tonsils, and if this operation is advised by an expert, I would say that the summer is the most favorable time; and the patient must allow a reasonable period to elapse in order that he may become accustomed to the new conditions. The real benefit after the operation is usually felt in about eight to twelve weeks.

The Uvula

Special mention must be made of uvula, as it is frequently mistaken for the soft palate, and a great deal of trouble has been caused through this misunderstanding.

The raising of the soft palate, to be beneficial, means a gentle arching of the veils of the soft palate, right and left of the uvula. This is, in part, one of the most essential elements of training of our vocal organs. It can be carried out successfully through suggestion of an "inner smile," and this to the beautifying of the entire voice; but where the uvula is mistaken for the soft palate and trained to be pulled up or raised, the entire top voice become small and insipid and cannot take on volume without the exercise of pressure, and the low and medium voice gets a peculiar covered or secondary sound, similar to that of a harmonica. In fact the raising of the uvula has an effect on the palate exactly opposite to the one desired. The importance lies in *raising the veils;* if the uvula drops, so much better, that being an indication that the important part of the palate is being arched.

We have had teachers who recommend the removing of the uvula for singers, one of the fads that come and go. If the uvula is inflamed, it is well to ask the advice of a doctor; but no special attention should be paid to this part of the soft palate. Methods training the directing of the vibrating air column against the hard palate frequently produce the same sound as voices trained to raise the uvula.

CHAPTER IV

The Production of the Voice or Tone

The production of the voice is a simple process and I prefer to describe it in brief so as to eliminate complications and facilitate definite understanding of later chapters.

The human voice may be classed as a wind-instrument, notwithstanding it has, for purpose of illustration, been compared to a violin. The operation of breath, vocal chords and resonating cavities is not unlike that of the corresponding features of a wood-wind instrument.

The human voice is produced thus:

We inhale until the lungs are comfortably filled, by a relaxed lowering movement of the abdominal wall; then we hesitate a moment (a fraction of a second) while the vocal chords automatically meet or close, thus resisting to a very slight degree the inhaled air; the abdominal muscles now slightly compress the air inhaled (a minimum fraction more than the resistance of the vocal chords). During exhalation, the vocal chords vibrate. These vibrations are directed through the form or shape assumed by the throat or vocal tube, and, through the transmission of the back wall of the throat and the spine, make the bone-structure of the head (skull) reverberate, or resound or resonate. The number of vibrations made by the vocal chords per second determine the pitch. The different forms of the vocal tube and positions of the larynx relative to the epiglottis produce the form of the tone or the vowel. This subject, as well as that of the mode of vocal chord vibration, will be taken up more definitely in other chapters.

Voice Classification

Voices, male and female, differ in range and color. The simplest classification in either sex is low, middle and high voice.

Male: Bass — Barytone — Tenor.
Female: Contralto — Mezzo — Soprano.

The male voices are then again divided into Basso profundo and Basse Cantante — Dramatic and Lyric Barytone and Dramatic and Lyric Tenor. These special classifications, however, are chiefly applicable to opera, and aside from the opera repertoire we can leave the voices of both sexes divided into three classes as stated above; low, middle and high.

The female voices are, however, for practicability better divided into Contralto, Mezzo Contralto and Mezzo Soprano; and Lyric and Dramatic Soprano and Coloratura Soprano.

The range is not the all important question that decides the class of voice; the tone color is equally important.

Only a most experienced ear can detect the subtle qualities that determine the classification of voices. Of course some voices are so decided that it needs no special judgment to place them correctly; but in many cases great care and judgment are required, and it is best to go slowly. Once a voice is wrongly classified, a great deal of time is lost. Dramatic Tenor and Lyric Barytone are frequently wrongly placed, as are also the Mezzo Soprano and Dramatic Soprano. It is always safer to leave the extreme high tones out of the question where there is lack of decision in the voice, and let *quality* be the predominant factor in deciding.

Vocal Technique

A fair knowledge of the vocal organs and their relative functions is a great help to the student in establishing facts.

The all-important point for the vocal beginner is to learn to *hear*. For instance, to learn to detect the difference between a dark tone-color and a covered tone; between breathy and brilliant singing. He must learn not to confuse volume with darkness, nor thinness with white or flat singing. Unbelievable errors exist on these points amongst singers; and frequently errors existing for years are almost immediately eradicated when the singer's sense of hearing is awakened.

The training of hearing pure vowels, pure in form and unmixed with consonant resonance, is also most important. I call it "consonant resonance" instead of "low nose resonance." This term will later be made more clear in the chapter on vowels and consonants and their construction.

The differences between good and bad tone production are caused by wrong adjustments of the vocal organs. As long as the singer does not *hear* he is at a standstill. The controlling and correcting of the physical error is minimized as soon as the student learns to hear correctly.

Let us say at this point regarding technique: being able to hear and recognize perfect and beautiful tone production produces a sense of satisfaction which has the effect of giving us confidence. Thus our endeavor in reaching technical perfection will be a combination of hearing and sensing the tone with comfort.

The adjustment of the movements of the physical organs, larynx, tongue, palate and breath-form are mostly described within the directions of width, depth and height; regarding the lips, the protrusion and relaxing of the same. These movements may be suggested but soon become under second nature's control when the sense of hearing is trained to discern the perfect qualities of the normally produced voice and thus only demands that the vocal organs perform their duty in Nature's way. We find this perfect function in vocal organs belonging to singers with phenomenal voices. So let us not try to improve upon Nature's ways of producing; rather let us ask her to help us over difficulties created by false human conception or misunderstanding of the art of singing.

Sense of Touch
or
The Feeling of the Tone

The term *sense of touch* is a new term to most singers. Sense of touch is a much neglected part of the training of students and the so often used suggestion of " feeling nothing when singing" is most misleading and at times dangerous. The vocal mind feels as well as hears. We would be at a great disadvantage if we could not *feel* the sensation of perfect singing. Having fixed it in our memory, it is a great help in repeating with security and confidence good results obtained.

It is useless to go to the extreme, as so many teachers do, of refusing to acknowledge any sensing of a tone, but continually to point out and suggest some intangible sensing of a forward or nasal position. These suggestions are misleading and leave the thinking student confused.

Tone production is caused by the physical attitude of our vocal organs. This physical attitude is felt and controlled through our hearing of the results. Therefore it is of the utmost importance that we learn to adjust the invisible singing organs in obedience to the demands of our ear. This can safely be done only by sensing the adjustment — in other words, *feeling the tone*.

The singer who experiences difficulties in producing vowels in different tone heights and refuses to investigate the physical discomfort that accompanies his vocalism under certain conditions, will never remedy these difficulties. He must learn to discover and acknowledge a wrong physical cause for vocal difficulties. Students who are not trained to do so, usually for want of knowledge on the teacher's part, are hopelessly at a standstill and are being encouraged to accept inferior results.

As has been said before, *width*, *depth* and *height* are the most essential to recognize and control.

These positions are the logical basis of all vowel production, and those who do not comprehend them and their relation to the formation of vowel tones, are often trying to fit squares into circles and *vice versa*. A logical, definite explanation followed by illustrative tone-production would, where the mind is not too antagonistic or the ear too far gone to recognize perfect tones, at once convince them of the truth regarding the feeling and hearing of *cause* and *effect*.

The foregoing statements regarding sense of touch are to make the student realize that error can be overcome only by analyzing its *cause* and that, as tone is a result of a physical adjustment mentally controlled, he cheats himself when he refuses to get at the actual cause.

The acquiring of the sense of touch is fairly divided between the mental and physical faculties, neither of the two alone will do all, but a happy and fair combination of the two branches of knowledge, with common sense and judgment, can work wonders.

CHAPTER V

Vocal Chord Mechanism — Register and Registers

The question naturally arises: Is it any benefit to the singer to understand the vocal chords and their working? I should reply that it depends upon the mind of the singer, and the knowledge of the teacher, as well as the latter's ability to explain and demonstrate. In my instruction I am guided by the talent of the pupil, and, as a rule, given ordinary intelligence, I regard a simple but correct understanding of the voice producers (vocal chords or vibratory organs) as beneficial. This knowledge helps to make the pupil more observing and sharpens his judgment as to cause and effect. Among my singing acquaintances are people who are entirely ignorant of this subject, and among my students are numbered those who are progressing splendidly without this knowledge. But these are special talents where the teacher must use judgment so as not to confuse the instinctive singing talent.

The vocal chords are commonly termed the **glottis**,— but this is incorrect, as glottis means the opening between the chords or vocal lips. The name " glottis " originated with Galen (130 A.D.) who made definite experiments in this direction, and found in the throat of pigs the larynx which he called " glottis." This name also designated the tongue of the instrument used at that time called the Aulos— similar to the Oboe, we surmise. Perhaps Galen meant the whole organ, the *larynx glottis* or *glottis laryngis*.

The name " vocal chord " does not indicate the existence of chords, strings or even bands, although they appear as such when viewed from above with the laryngoscope. But these chords are like lips, appearing from the inside as folds, one in each side of the larynx horizontally extended. One end is fastened to the middle of the thyroid cartilage, the other to the cricoid cartilage and the arytenoids and these again ecentrically socketed,— permitting the opening and closing of the chords.

PLATE 3

Larynx (inner side view) omiting muscle sinews excepting vocal chords. Shows what degree the vocal chords shorten in the Low, Medium, and High Voice. Showing that the singing in the High Voice is not the tightening of the chords but rather the shortening of the vibration part equal to the shortening of the string on a stringed instrument for the producing of higher notes.

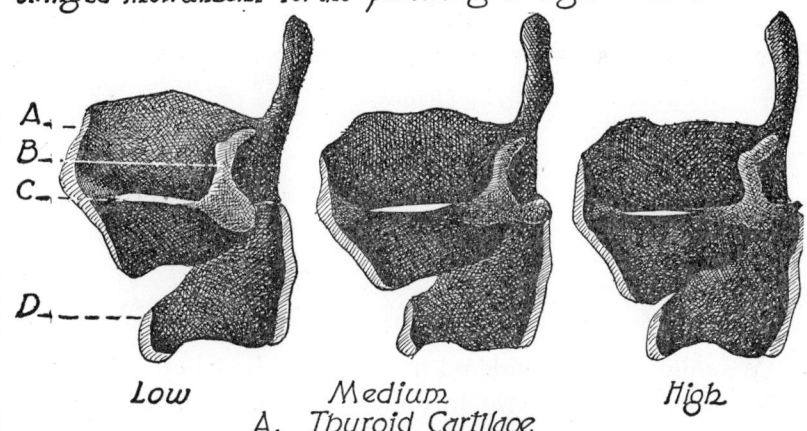

Low   Medium   High

A. Thyroid Cartilage
B. Arytenoid Cartilage
C. Vocal Chords
D. Cricoid Cartilage

The closing necessary for the chords to resist the slightly compressed air in the lungs from sudden escape, is effected by a backward leaning movement of the cricoid as well as the turning of the arytenoids. The chords closed resist the air,— when the compression overcomes the resistance an explosion follows. The air having found an exit is less compressed and the chords close again. These explosions take place many times a second and their rapid succession impresses the ear as a sound or one tone. The more vibrations per second the higher the pitch. The ear cannot distinguish a tone of less than sixteen vibrations per second (which is only noise). A musical tone requires at least forty vibrations per second or the intonation cannot be registered. The physical upward limit of our hearing sensation is about four thousand vibrations per second. Intonated tones remain between forty and four thousand vibrations.

The following table shows the number of vibrations within the usual seven octaves in which it is apparent that the octave vibrates twice as much as its ground tone or *tonica*.

Octave.

1	2	3	4	5	6	7
C	C	C	C	C	C	C-B
33	66	132	264	528	1056	2112-3960

Middle Octave.

C	D	E	F	G	A	B	C
264	297	330	352	390	440	495	528

We might have wondered how it could be possible for the vocal lips to assume such a high rate of vibration. The lips do not vibrate through independent movements but through recurrences, the innate elasticity causing the return to the normal position. At each explosion a small amount of air passes, leaving below the chords a vacuum which is constantly replenished from the compressed air in the lungs. This vacuum brings the chords together again until the air pressure is great enough to sever them. These continued explosions produce the sound or tone.

At this point a reference to *registers* is in place. A register means a certain number of tones produced after one and the same mode of vibration (the term "register" has been taken over from the organ). We have what is called a pure chest voice in which the vocal lips meet at longer and thicker proportions, as shown in the illustration. These heavy vibrations of the lower voice through reverbrations of the expanded windpipe, transmit vibrations in the chest. This sensation is always present in male voices, but only obvious in the lower part of female voices, where it gives the tone-color a masculine quality. As long as these proportions remain in contact after each vibration the tone has the same quality. In order that the voice may ascend, an increase in the number of vibrations is necessary, and to accomplish this the vocal lips are compelled to reduce their length. This is fundamental with all stringed instruments,— the shorter the distance that the string bridges, the higher the number of vibrations. This principle holds true with the vocal chords. This is also seen in the illustration where the difference in the opposite turning position of the cricoid cartilage towards the thyroid cartilage denotes an increased or decreased expansion in the vibrating part of the vocal chords.

If we train each of these so-called registers to its full extent, in producing the next register a sudden change of quality is apparent. The sudden disappearance of volume and change in quality is met with between the low and the medium voice in mezzo and contralto voices, although in some cases the change appears between the medium and the high voice. This developing of registers in tone production cannot lead to artistic results. We must sing with one register throughout the entire range of the voice and so balance the adjustment of the vocal chords that they do not *suddenly* divert into another quality, but do so gradually. This process is also more advantageous as it equalizes the tone-color throughout the entire range.

The important place to balance or equalize, in the beginning, is between C and G. The vowel *e* helps us in doing this, but all vowels must be used later on. If the vocal chords are over-adjusted the voice in consequence will be too thick and will break or change in quality and sound dull, but if correctly adjusted it will go through the medium and even to the high voice without alteration. The principle upon which the one-register scale is constructed is based upon a thin adjustment of the low and medium voice, but omitting the so-called pure chest-quality, except in the extreme deep voice where it joins automatically when the medium is brought down, not causing, however, the voice to become insipid in quality or volume. A nasally produced voice encounters great difficulty in finding the tone-color which gives the one-register scale. In other words the one-register scale means merely a distribution of qualities which otherwise would define or separate a voice into three or more registers, viz., low, medium and high. As seen in the illustration (Plate 3), the low voice has the largest vibrating adjustment of the vocal chords, the medium, less, and the high, the least. In order that the low voice be brilliant and clear it should have skull resonance and the high voice should have a round but brilliant color — that is to say, the high voice should not sound disconnected. The medium voice should possess both of these qualities, uniting the high and the low.

The training of the one-register scale has best resulted from a knowledge of vowel combinations. The vowels have a definite effect upon the larynx position as well as upon the adjustment of the vocal lips. With this knowledge the vocal chords can be trained to produce with ease the one-register scale with normal uniform tone quality throughout the range on all vowels, the top voice being rounded, but not covered.

PLATE 4

Fig. 1 — Open glottis for inhaling. male.
a.
b.
c.

Fig. 2 — Partly closed glottis - falsetto. male.

Fig. 3 — Closed glottis spoken voice. male.
note:

Fig. 4 — Closed vocal chords sung low. voice male.

Fig. 5 — Closure of chords maxium voice. male.

a. represents epiglottis also forward position of larynx in throat.
b. indicates vocal chords.
c. indicates position of arytenoids.

These drawings facilitate in visualizing changes from low to high voice in vibratory surface or length of vocal chords that vibrate. (this knowledge only for those interested - but does not teach singing).

Fig. 6 — male.

Fig. 7 — mezzo-soprano. Shows change of vocal chord

Fig. 8 — soprano. Shows closure of vocal chords high voice.

Fig. 10 — coloratura soprano. Shows closure of vocal chords on high staccato D natural.

Closure of vocal chords - high voice. Closure between med. and high voice.

(29)

As seen from the foregoing, this theory is based on the balance of adjustment and tone-color, or breath without pressure.

There is yet another method for the producing of tones,—the so-called *falsetto* or open-glottis method in which the chords do not meet, thereby causing the emmited tone to resemble that of a flute and eventually that of a ventriloquist. Such a production will never develop volume nor possess artistic value. This open-glottis voice can, at best, be used only as a substitute for pianissimo and cannot be united with any other voice unless change of timbre, break or hiccough follows. Female voices, notably German sopranos, using this so-called head-tone, invariably sing off the key.

The register with the closed glottis can be trained to perfect production no matter how soft the attack may be. But the singer to obtain this result, must be guided most carefully and judiciously from the very first training. And, all-important, the student must never press nor force his voice or this ideal condition will never be reached.

Beautiful singing with a graceful and pleasing *diminuendo* and *crescendo* is very rare. Haste to achieve results, lack of knowledge on the part of the teachers and overestimation of mediocre talent on the side of the pupil are to blame for many damaged voices and disappointed singers.

There is a great difference in voices and talents. A few individuals are fortunate enough to be born with a facility for acquiring *pianissimo* quickly, but usually there are deficiencies to offset this advantage. Voices which are over-burdened in the general attack and those that have been placed above the natural *tessitura* usually experience the greatest difficulty in producing *pianissimo*.

The Attack

The term *Attack*, as we use it in singing, means simply the starting of the tone. A wrong attack is sometimes called the stroke of the glottis. This term originated with Manual Garcia, who explained the attack of the tone as a " neat stroke of the glottis," but at the same time warning against the shock of the chest. Garcia was severely criticized on this point by those who did not definitely understand him. Some singers who exaggerated the stroke of the glottis soon suffered from congestion of the vocal chords; but those who knew what the great master meant, drew benefit from his suggestion, the " neat stroke of the glottis."

But let me make it clear to my readers what the term *attack* means as applied to singing. We have about four kinds of attacks that we may clasify:

1st. The *over-balanced* attack, called glottis-stroke, where the vocal chords are being pinched together stronger than the minimum, and which consequently demands a stronger compression of air to set the too tight closed vocal chords into vibration.

2nd. The *under-balanced* attack, where the breath flows through the glottis and the vocal chords gradually close over the stream of exhaled breath until they commence vibrating. This kind of attack is meant to counteract tendencies to forcing, but robs the tone of its momentum. I have, however, heard singers who have worked out this theory most wonderfully, but the duration of their career was shorter than normal. Among these singers we can mention Gerster, Kempfner and Nikish.

3rd. The attack where the student is led to think that the tone starts with a slight nasal humming sound previous to the starting of the tone proper. This attack leads to the most unfortunate complications, and eventually directs the mind of the singer away from the actual conditions of a perfect attack, as compared with the two previously mentioned methods.

The perfect attack is better described as the moment that always appears between the execution of a physical action resulting from a mental demand. I call this moment, no matter how short the point of hesitation, or the form of preparation it involves, the *breath-form* in correspondence to the tone-power, tone-height, vowel-form and tone-color. All of these four qualities necessary for perfect tone production adjust themselves automatically if we are taught to think before we sing, in the absolutely logical way, and in any attack the principal holds good, and the result will never fail.

This training of mental automotive control over the vocal organs should be begun with the first lesson and the teacher must observe very closely and not consider range in the beginning. Range is the least consideration after the medium voice takes on perfect one-register tone-quality.

These four points that automatically adjust themselves if we think before we sing, are very simple. We mentally hear the volume we want to produce, and if our breathing organs are free and normal, they automatically inhale through relaxation what the mind demands of them, the throat assumes the form of the vowel subconsciously, the tone-height is mentally adjusted, and the tone-color takes on the expression of the meaning of the text, according to the intensity of the thoughts to be expressed either dramatically or poetically. And the attack of the vocal chords or their closing, becomes an absolutely subconscious movement of which we are relieved, as the mind adjusts all such conditions for us.

CHAPTER VI

Abnormal Breathing

Breathing, I think, is more often misunderstood than any other branch of the art of singing and in consequence more frequently abused; surely, here, the blind lead the blind more often than not.

There is a great difference between training the different parts of the breathing organs to perform athletic " stunts " and training them to work in harmony with the voice.

I find, always, that those students who pride themselves in being able to resist the pressure of two or more of their strong friends by stiffening the abdominal muscles, are better forcers of the voice than producers of free, floating tone. Voices produced with overburdened breath pressure become wooden, explosive, off-key, and lacking in carrying power.

How often we hear untrained voices produce lovely free tones throughout the entire voice, with no thought of the breath or breathing. When we hear these same voices after a year or two of bad training, we find that they have become harsh, unmusical and forced. Too often this is the case and frequently for no other reason than a wrong conception of breathing.

You can always feel certain that those singers who produce phenomenal tones are not those who force the breath and get red in the face.

If students would use a bit of logic they would realize that to force or push the breath means to compel the throat to resist unnecessary pressure.

In rare cases it would be wise to train a student in breathing gymnastics, but then only as a general benefit to health, not as a direct use in singing.

The old Italians said, "He who knows how to breathe knows how to sing." But remember, they did not say, "He who can lift tons of weight with his breath knows how to sing."

The moment we deviate in the slightest from Nature's lines of breathing, we sing incorrectly. Breath and tones are so automatically united that we must use the utmost care to avoid any overburden or pressure of breath, or the voice will surely reflect wrong results at once. And if this overbalance of breath becomes a habit, the singer soon loses his keen judgment as to his own tone-production, becomes a slave to the habit of forcing and from day to day, instead of developing his voice into an art that is perfect, he deteriorates.

These remarks are intended to encourage the student to think for himself. Only intelligent self-criticism can bring an artist to the height of perfection.

Breathing exercises where students hold their breath as long as possible and then exhale slowly, producing hissing sounds or similar noises, are absolutely useless, if not detrimental. The control and economy of the breath in singing is an entirely different process. The muscles never hold back the breath from escaping, but the vibrators, or the vocal chords, control and convert the slowly flowing breath into resonance or voice, and the least possible pressure means balance and control and economy of breath.

The real controller of breath expenditure, from a mental and physical viewpoint, is the *tone* — the perfect, clear and undiffused tone. And this tone can be found only when the breathing organs work perfectly and naturally, controlled through our sense of hearing, but never by any hold or lifting or pressure of any muscles or group of muscles of the breathing organs.

We often hear the words, "breath control." Breath

controlled by the holding or drawing in or pushing out of any group of muscles must, at best, be an unnatural performance.

Normal Breathing

Preliminary to a complete understanding of normal breathing, let us get a picture in our minds of the breathing organs. The organs that perform in singing are those that perform at the first issue of life after birth, so I dare state that there ought to be a natural and normal way of using them.

The lungs hold the air while singing. The principle of the filling of the lungs remains the same in tone-production as in ordinary breathing, the difference being that the exhaled breath during tone-production is being converted into tone through the vibrations resulting in resonance through the mechanical action of the vocal chords. The vocal chords then form the resistance or control of the breath exhaled while converting it into tone. Consequently it is the tone which controls and distributes the breath; the breath is not controlled directly by any group of muscles, but automatically through the tone. The development of the breathing organs cannot grow rationally unless judged by the tone. It is the tone that tells our ear if we are using our vocal organs, and breath correctly or not. So therefore, directly or indirectly, the tone is and must be the first and ultimate controller of the exhaling of the breath. Never forget that the beautiful tone is for the ear and must not be distorted by any forced physical attitude. We have, to our sorrow, too many exponents of the brute art of shouting.

Let us look at the construction of our breathing apparatus and remember that the new-born human being of

PLATE 5

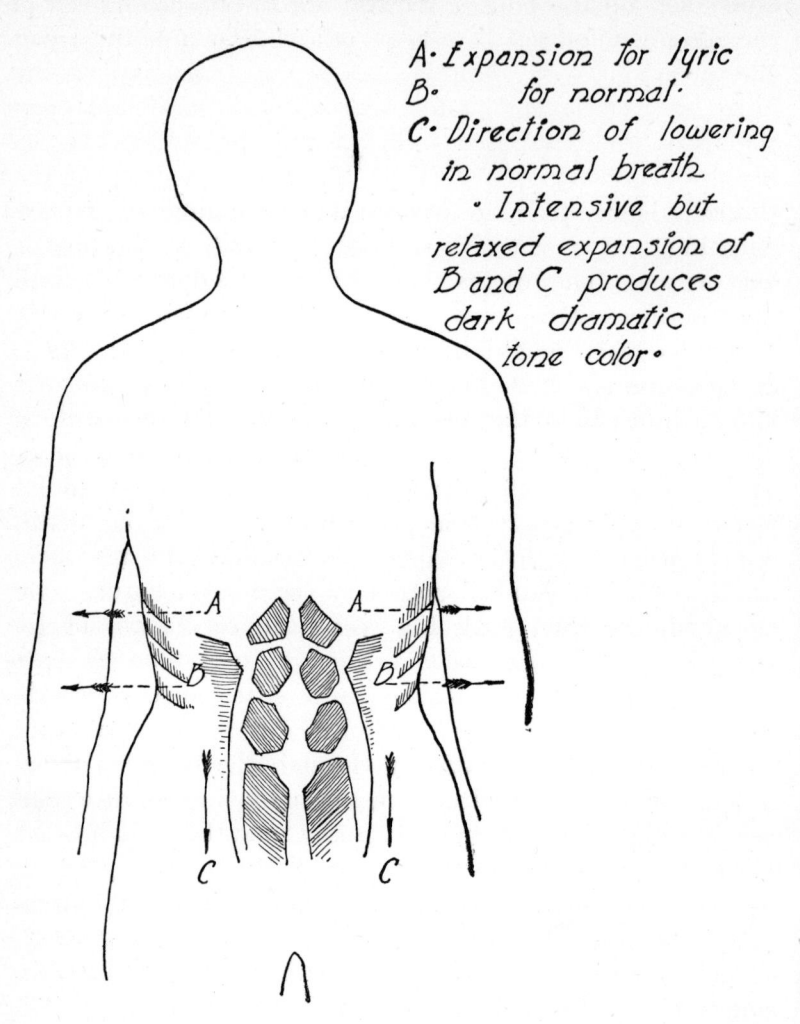

A. Expansion for lyric
B.   for normal.
C. Direction of lowering in normal breath
 · Intensive but relaxed expansion of B and C produces dark dramatic tone color.

either sex breathes by a relaxed downward movement of the abdomen and not by a heaving and raising of the upper chest. And why? Simply because the capacity of the lungs is more dependent upon their lower part than upon the upper, and Nature has built the chest pointed and tapering upward, with loose floating ribs at the bottom of the thorax. Here the lungs rest upon the diaphragm and the diaphragm in turn rests upon the digestive tract which is held in place by the spine at the back, the abdominal wall in front, and on the sides by the dorsal or hip-basket below.

Now Nature has taught us the process of filling the lungs by relaxation sidewise and forward and the lowering of the abdomen. This lowers the diaphragm which then, in turn, fills the lungs. This process repeats itself through life — while awake in even rhythm; while asleep, as (1) inhalation, (2) repose, (3) exhalation; while in singing the breath is subordinate to the demands of the mind which instinctively distributes it to produce the phrases demanded by the music performed. As has been mentioned often before, the less breath expended, the more perfect the tone — the more diffused or breathy the tone, the more air or breath is being wasted without producing results. Consequently the prime requisite of normal breathing is to learn to recognize the perfectly vibrating tone through its perfect resonance. This accomplished, we are launched into the first principles of normal breathing which is automatically set up when we inhale through relaxation rather by methods so commonly and wrongly taught by which the student, contrary to nature, draws in the abdomen, raises the chest, sings unnaturally and looks anything but natural.

The first exercise in listening to perfect resonance indirectly trains the valve or the vocal chords to close and control the exhalation without waste. The repetition of each exercise or tone is training in itself. The gradual extension of the scales or combinations of tones instinctively trains the breathing organs to inhale the amount of breath that the mind automatically directs. This is a small amount because the proper tone exhausts almost no breath. Only the wrongly produced voice needs an abnormal amount of breath which overtaxes the breathing organs at the expense of overburdened vocal chords and an unnatural physical attitude and poise of the singer. Do you not remember a time in your own experience in singing when you forgot how you breathed — perhaps did not even notice that you took a breath? — and still you sang better than when you prepared that big breath with the full chest, the powerful diaphragm, and felt blown up like a balloon. Singers with a breathing method like a pumping apparatus, ask yourselves this question; then use your common sense and go back to Nature and, perhaps sooner than you think, you will find some of those lovely tone qualities that first encouraged your study of singing. Tone qualities are too often killed by absurd and forced methods that are in absolute contradiction of Nature's intentions. Think of the relaxed movements of the trunk of the body in the process of inhalation, which creates the energy used for singing, as automatic return movements which, automatically repeated and instinctively controlled, constitute the *Art of Normal Breathing.*

Never force the breath up against the lower part of the lungs, as it raises the tract of the lungs with the windpipe and presses directly against the larynx. If the larynx is exposed to pressure it becomes fixed, resisting this pressure and loses the facility to assume the differences in position for the different vowels and tone-colors. The singer who forces breath is frequently reduced to one tone-color and one size of voice unless he *forgets himself* and breathes naturally. As all tone production is a result of inhalation, learn to inhale in a relaxed condition, or the return movement, exhalation, will be forced and react injuriously upon the tone production. The relaxing movement of the entire trunk of the body, with the sidewise movement, expands the floating ribs, the downward and outward

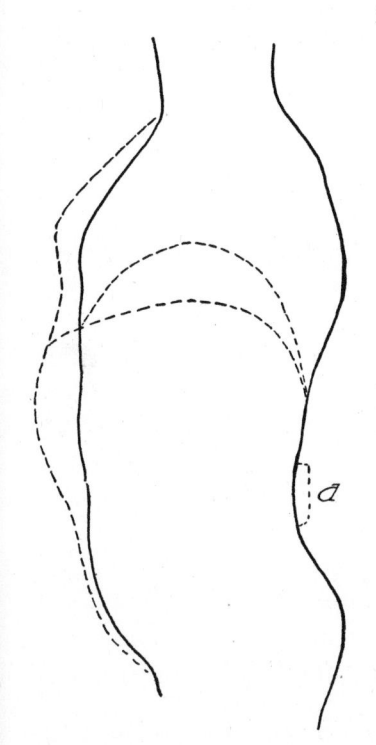

PLATE 6

Reinforced breath dangerous because the upper part of abdomen protrudes forcing against diaphragm instead of automatically creating balance between chest and diaphragm.

direction of the abdominal wall lowers the diaphragm, and as a result the lungs fill with air, and the chest instinctively takes on its expansion according to the amount of breath inhaled. The unison of these movements through **relaxation form the principle of** *Normal Breathing.*

Breath-form Relative to Tone-color

The term *breath-form* will seem new to some of my readers. In the construction of vowels we use the term *form*, we speak of *width* and *depth*. We have noticed that *width* is predominant in the bright vowels; that dark vowels are dependent upon the *depth* of the larynx and that the neutral vowel *a* (ah) is a combination or a tone representing a combination of the bright and dark vowel qualities in one. We might well call the neutral vowel *a* (ah) the *normal* vowel, as it presents qualities of both *width* and *depth*.

The normal breath-form presents a combination of width and depth, that is, a certain amount of broadening of the lower ribs and a corresponding amount of lowering of the abdominal wall in the act of inhaling. If, now, the width of the breath-form should be augmented and the depth diminished in proportion, our tone-color would assume a brighter, perhaps we may call it a more lyric tone-color. Now, if we should augment the depth of our breath-form by lowering the abdomen and decrease the width in proportion, our tone-color would in consequence assume a darker color. We will state simply the reasons for these conditions in a logical way.

The lowering of the abdomen lowers the diaphragm and the lungs, consequently the windpipe and the larynx; and this lowering is the natural formation of dark tone-color, as we prove through the lowering of the larynx in producing the dark vowel *oo*.

A broadening of the floating ribs raises or levels the diaphragm against the lower part of the lungs, raising the same, and in consequence, the windpipe and the larynx approach the higher larynx positions for the bright vowels *e*, *a*, etc.

From the foregoing we see a very close relation between vowels dark and bright relative to tone-color dark and bright.

Our aim is first to normalize tone-color on all of the different vowels. In this way we create normality of breath-form in relation to tone-color.

At this point it would be reasonable to ask the question,—Should we not train breath-form relative to dark or bright tone-color instead of only singing normally? This question is not easy to answer. The singer who possesses the talent of coloring his songs from the interpretative viewpoint gained through an understanding of the text, instinctively uses the correct breath-form and does not need any special training further than a knowledge of the effect of breath-form upon the tone-color relative to augmented depth and width of the same; but I have at times found it extremely beneficial with certain voices to train breath-form. However, in most cases it becomes instinctive to the singer once normality has been reached and understood, as it is instinctive and natural for us to color our voices in spoken words according to the demands of different situations. The difference in our greeting of a friend and of a person whom we dislike or prefer not to meet, is a simple indication of instinctive change of tone-color according to differences in mental or physical attitudes.

The analyzing of breath-form could be made very complicated, but for our uses it is best to remain within the most simple terms and classify the term breath-form as follows:

Bright or *lyric*. — The width of the floating ribs is the determining factor in inhaling.

The *dark* or *dramatic*. — The predominating movement is a lowering of the abdominal tract.

The *normal*. — An equal, comfortable and combined lowering and widening of both the floating ribs and the abdomen.

It is to be remembered that the above described breath-forms must be created in the *inhalation*, as the result in singing becomes apparent in the return movement or exhalation. Inhaling for the lyric quality and then lowering the abdomen while singing would not give a satisfactory result. Inhaling by lowering the breath-form and then broadening or pulling in the abdomen is often used to emphasize or reinforce high tones, which can be done if great judgment is used; but if abused or made the usual way of producing the high voice, the tone becomes hard and forced and the *pianissimo* soon disappears or becomes breathy.

In closing this subject I repeat that the training of what is usually termed the *breath* — breathing methods of different kinds — also called breath-control from a muscular viewpoint, at best can only lead to complications and confusion if trained separately from *tone-production*. To learn to breathe normally for singing involves training and development in connection with tone-production, the breathing being part of the production. But the tone, judged through hearing, is the real control. Range, facility, pure vowels easily produced, variety of volume, independence of volume in tone-production, are tests for the singer that determine if he is trained correctly or not. If a voice is not able to pass these tests of perfect technique there is an error somewhere or a radically wrong conception of the art of singing. Singers who push with their breath at times cleverly produce a *crescendo;* but a *diminuendo* after the *crescendo* would be a fairer test. The singer who realizes that the tone, through a perfect training of the sense of hearing, controls the breath, and not *vice versa* is on the simpler and safer road to the perfect art of singing. Singing should be controlled through the hearing and not through any direct group of muscles expanding or contracting. If we depart from the lines which Nature has laid down for us we shall not succeed. If we allow the contracting and

PLATE 7

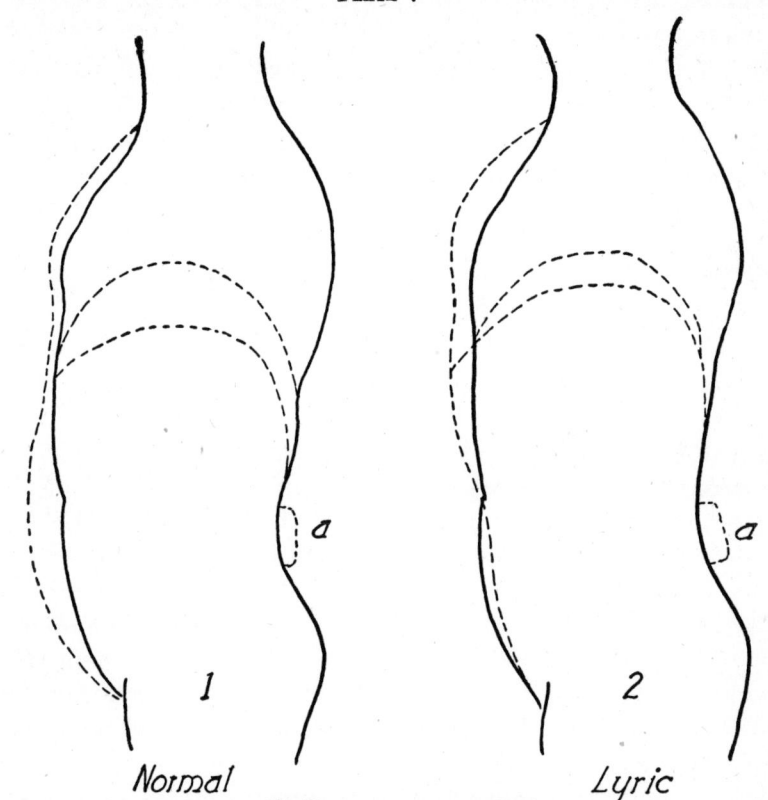

        1   2
     Normal   Lyric
       • Both exaggerated •

a•   Point of relaxation in small of back
    from where breathing starts•
        Normal breath form can be changed
    to lyric by drawing in on abdomen and
    expanding ribs; but not always advisable
    as spoken of in the chapter on
    Breath Form Relative To Tone Color•

(43)

expanding of our breathing organs to gradually and instinctively develop with our perfecting of tone-production, our eventual art will be a far more complete art. Where the singer starts out with big reinforced tones that only lead to forcing or where he depends upon volume to produce tone, his *pianissimo* and *diminuendo* become less possible and soon impossible.

Support

Support is a term often used in regard to singing but not always definitely understood. Usually we hear the word *support* in relation to breathing. But to make its meaning more clear, I will go so far as to say that support of the voice from the viewpoint of practical singing is more a *sensation* than anything else; it is, in fact, a result of other conditions, concerned mainly with the vocal chords. All the breathing, holding and otherwise regulated movements can never be *supported* until the vocal chords vibrate perfectly and convert the vibrations into perfect resonance without waste of breath. Then can we speak of support; and here I would like to add in that a case of perfection — balanced support — the moment we have inhaled what we need for our tone-production, the vocal chords automatically close in the articulation of our vowel attack or diction in text. This moment between inhaling and producing, which I call the moment or point of hesitation, is the all-important factor in creating the *sensation* so often termed support. The moment the tone is articulated the flow of breath is held back by the closed vibrating vocal chords and this creation of resistance is the sensation termed support, but great care must be taken that this does not, through carelessness, become pushing instead of supporting. We could justly say, the feeling of support is a sense of security resulting from the functions of hearing and feeling working in unison.

Review on Breathing

Summarizing the subjects of **Abnormal Breathing,** the **Art of Normal Breathing** and **Breath-form Relative to Tone-color,** we make the statement that the different breathing methods termed Abdominal, Intercostal and Diaphragmatic are closely related to each other,— in fact could not logically be separated. Any of these named methods, or all of them, if cultivated separately for the purpose of performing tests of muscular strength, such strength, if applied to the voice as so-called "support," would prevent the tone from responding with perfect freedom. Whether our viewpoint be tone supported by the breath or the breath controlled by the tone, if the least amount of overbalance or pressure should enter our tone-production, the result would, to some degree, be forced and the vibratory organs or vocal chords could not perform automatically while compelled to resist overburdening of the breath. The normal tone-color adjusts the normal breathing and, if trained in connection with the tone as the controlling factor of our singing, we come closer to Nature's intentions. The amount of breath is physically adjusted in obedience to our mind's command, as we instinctively regulate our stride in crossing a space like a ditch or any distance greater than that of our customary step.

In singing, the important part is inhalation. We inhale what our mind demands for the producing of our exercise; or, in text, we also inhale the expression, the tone-color, that our mind desires to express; that is, if we treat our text from the viewpoint of its meaning, and not as empty words fitting a melody. If the basis of this inhalation is normal, the thousand different shades that the perfect art demands of the singer will readily appear; but if our art is bound by a preparatory raising of the chest, a pulling here or a pushing there, we are, from the very beginning, hampered in obtaining freedom and naturalness as a basis for growth in our art of singing. Nature teaches us to breathe through the nose, so do not depart from that rule. I realize the great difficulty of overcoming the error of mouth-breathing, which is almost impossible where the singer has become accustomed to it; but determination in exercises can overcome this. Do not forget that closing the lips tightly while learning to breathe through the nose is dangerous, as then the chest heaves, the breathing is apt to be noisy, and the abdominal part of Nature's breathing apparatus does not work automatically. By breathing through the nose, the lips slightly apart, and with a relaxing of the whole abdominal tract and lower ribs, starting from the small of the back, our lungs will fill more readily and with less effort than in any other way of breathing. If we accustom ourselves in our technique to mentally inhale the *vowel*, the *power*, the *duration* and the *height* of our exercise, we shall soon observe the ease with which our breathing organs will perform for us, — in fact, the diaphragm, lower ribs, and abdomen, will all work automatically in harmony, helping one another without overtaxing any part of the breathing organs. It is all-important to realize that the expanding or raising of the chest must never be a direct movement but always a result of making room for the gradual filling of the lungs through the abdominal relaxed expansion.

The method of developing the breathing organs under the training of normal breathing controlled through the result of the tone and, consequently, the hearing, is a far safer and less complicated one than any other method of breathing, and I daresay that the logic of this method would appeal to the mind of any person not antagonistic to naturalness and normality.

CHAPTER VII

Pianissimo and Forte — Crescendo and Diminuendo

To many singers, probably to most singers, *Pianissimo Crescendo* and *Diminuendo* are difficult to achieve.

To describe the actual processes engaged in producing these effects would, perhaps, be confusing to most singers, for the reason that few have studied the construction of the vocal and related organs. I do not believe that a knowledge of the vibratory surfaces of the vocal chords and the changes that are involved in producing a *crescendo* or *diminuendo* would necessarily be of value to a student seeking to cultivate *pianissimo*. But it may not be unproductive of good results if we present the matter in as simple a picture as possible, for the study of those who are especially interested in causes. First, consider the glottis vibrating while producing a tone of normal size. (Vocal chord mode of vibrating described elsewhere.) If the tone increases in size, the longitude (the length of the part of the vocal lips vibrating) of the vocal lips also increases and in consequence the corresponding amplitude of the vibrations (this corresponding to the amount of the opening of the glottis between consecutive vibrations). A *diminuendo* or return from a *crescendo* or, in fact, any size of voice towards *pianissimo*, is dependent upon the reverse movement, — a most simple mechanical action to understand.

But the far more important points for the student to understand are the errors that prevent the voice from producing these perfect tests of technique. I justly place this chapter after the one on breathing because these finer technical points in our art of singing are usually directly lost through wrong or forced breathing and wrongly used nasal resonance. If a tone produced in normal size is to be increased in volume and the intensity of the breath is being increased by muscular pressure instead of being instinctively or automatically controlled and guided through the sense of hearing, the *crescendo* would be forced or overbalanced, and a *diminuendo* would be impossible or would be dull or breathy, as the overburdening of the *crescendo* would react on the *diminuendo* and continually have to be counteracted. This would create an uncomfortable feeling for the singer as well as a most discouraging dullness in the *diminuendo*. (Inability to attack softly on high tones on different vowels can be traced to the lack of the all-important knowledge, for the beginner, of discriminating through the sense of hearing. Success in producing the finer parts of vocal technique is a result of a perfected ABC of the art of singing, and it is useless to attempt the finished art without this preliminary knowledge and training. I make these statements at this point, as experience has taught me the impossibility of correcting errors where fundamental knowledge is lacking.) Therefore in order to control a *crescendo* and a *diminuendo* it is all-important that the singer's ear be sufficiently trained in keeping exact vowel-form and tone-color fixed in his memory or he will soon mistake *crescendo* for an increase in darkness and a *diminuendo* for, perhaps, an exaggerated thinning out of the voice bordering on diffused, breathy or falsetto tone. Therefore, again I must state that before a pupil has learned to hear with perfect discrimination, all studies of differences of size in tone-production during one phrase or one breath, would be of little definite benefit; but if this work or part of the study is taken up at the proper time and with the proper understanding, it gives courage and pleasure and directly benefits the student's rendition of songs.

The thing to guard against most in the studying of the

increase and decrease in the size of the voice is a darkening of the tone-color with the increase of the voice and a tendency to diffuse or go towards a breathy quality in decreasing the size of the voice. Guard against muscular breath pressure; it compels the vocal chords to thicken and this thickness of attack is an obstacle to all finer points in our art of singing.

CHAPTER VIII

Nasal Support

It will be noted that warning against wrong use or overuse of nasal resonance appears in several of our chapters and consequently it is not out of place to devote some special mention of this important factor in regard to nasal singing, pro and con. The French language presents more nasal resonance than any other universal language and it would be absurd to say anything detrimental against this wonderful language, which, when sung or spoken by natives or those thoroughly understanding its intricate construction, abounds in color, sonority, grace and elegance.

But the English speaking nations have an entirely different nasality in speaking, almost a nasal twang; which is a detriment to the singing voice directly, because it obstructs head resonance — indirectly because the keener sense of hearing is impaired by constant wrong use or abuse of our English language. That English is equal to any language in beauty and richness of color and vowel combinations has been demonstrated by many singers of high standing.

As has been said several times before, natural nasality is found in the largest degree in our nasal consonants M and N; other consonants, as explained in different chapters, are mostly singable, that is, the line of resonance is not definitely broken or changed in color as in M and N. No tone can be sung entirely without nasal resonance and only when the nasality appears in such proportion as definitely to color the vowels and their resonance, does it become a detriment to the beauty of the voice. We have singers and methods that teach this nasal quality to an extent unbearable. Sometimes we hear — " use your nose and save your throat," " feel your vocal chords in your nose." All of these suggestions, no matter how well they are meant, lead to serious complications, the most common of which is forcing. I could here make this comparison — The nasal tone is equivalent in resonance to the soft pedal quality of a piano. While the soft pedal is applied it would be impossible to produce a big tone because the singing quality of the instrument is being deadened. It is the same with voices that use as a method, the nasal resonance as a guiding or supporting quality in their singing. Italian singers differ mostly from singers of other nations on this point of nasality.

As our treatise on the voice is meant to a greater extent as a key to the understanding of the indisputable superiority of Italian singers, I feel justified in pointing out the dangers arising from wrong use of nasality.

Larynx, Palate, Tongue and Mouth

The *larynx, palate; tongue* and *mouth* are so closely related to one another that a brief description, aside from the numerous allusions to them in other chapters, will not be out of place.

The larynx is the sound-box and the container of the vibratory organs. The opening from the larynx forms the part of the throat that we feel to be opening when lowering and loosely broadening the root of the tongue on the neutral and dark vowels and when arching the tongue high on the bright vowels. Here we mold our vowels and, by arching the veils of the palate, we prevent the vowel sound from entering the nose, thus keeping our vowels pure and full of head-resonance. By lowering the palate we permit sound to enter the nasal cavity, thus producing the different consonants with the additional help of the tip of the tongue, hard palate, teeth and lips. Thus we see that our singing is mainly a combination of larynx, tongue, palate and lips working in obedience to the demand and command of the mind or hearing. So do not let us shirk the little trouble it gives us to know truthfully the combined working of these organs. They are the only organs that require to be trained in the cultivation of the true singing voice; and a thorough knowledge of their combined functions, together with the natural way of breathing, constitute the Art of Singing.

CHAPTER IX

Vowels and Consonants

The vowel is the part of the word which we sustain; the consonant, the part beginning or finishing the word or dividing the syllables. Some words, however, begin or terminate with vowels, but this does not concern our chapter.

It will be most practical to consider these two classes of sound from the viewpoint of their physical construction.

In the first place we must know why a sound is a vowel or why it is a consonant.

All resonant sounds have two kinds of resonance, and two only.

Vowel resonance, which is not directed into the nasal cavity nor obstructed in any other way.

Consonant resonance which *is* directed into the nasal cavity or is obstructed in other ways to be described in the classifications.

If consonants were not nasal or otherwise obstructive our sounds would have no contrast; consequently to make our sounds, vowels or consonants, distinct, each must be produced in its proper way.

The obvious difference between vowels and consonants in acoustic effect is that vowels are brilliant and consonants dull.

If we produce a tone with our mouth closed we call it humming. Observe that humming is not capable of producing vowel forms nor brilliancy, which proves that Nature does not intend us to produce brilliant tones by humming; and it also proves that the dullness which is characteristic of the consonant, is caused by its nasal quality.

The vowel-forms register differently upon our sense of hearing because of the difference in the forms of the tone-waves.

If the throat were not able to change its form, we could not utter the different vowels. Our tone in such case, would be an instrumental tone. And here, we note that the voice can do what no instrument can do, — it can produce sounds of different form, color and class of resonance by reason of its ability to change the form or mold of the producing organ.

In analyzing the vowel-forms we resort to the directions which the forms of the inner and outer mouth assume while we produce or mold our tone into vowel-form. These directions are most simply understood as increase and decrease in width and depth.

Our bright vowels are dependent upon a broader form of the inner-mouth and at the back, a higher standing tongue.

We often say that the tongue is an organ impossible to control. Many a teacher, in an effort to cover up his own ignorance, teaches his pupils not to think about the tongue. This may suffice in some cases, but rarely.

Students who are not taught to hear the difference between pure vowels and vowels produced with low nose resonance experience great difficulty at first in controlling the tongue, but the moment the ear detects the difference between right and wrong, the tongue always becomes obedient.

The reason why the tongue positions change from high to low, or, perhaps better said, from concave to convex, is not usually understood.

The vibrations of the vocal chords convert the air into a flow of tone-waves, often called "the vibrating air-column." The form of these waves is to a great extent controlled by the epiglottis.

The epiglottis stands perpendicularly against the root of the tongue. The higher the tongue is at the back, the more perpendicular is the epiglottis and consequently of less interference to the emission of the tone-waves. Vowels formed in this way are termed "bright vowels" as $\bar{e}$, $\breve{\imath}$, $\breve{a}$, $\breve{e}$. The moment the tongue alters to a concave position the epiglottis leans over the glottis and the sound-waves are rounded. These rounded vowel-forms are termed neutral vowel-forms as a (ah), and the dark vowel forms as a (aw), $\bar{o}$ and $\overline{oo}$.

From the foregoing we see that where a tongue position does not correspond with the vowel demanded of us, we are uncomfortable in our production or we must compromise and sing impure vowels.

Students who for general vocalization use the dark forms, naturally will feel awkward producing bright vowels or *vice versa*.

Therefore the all-important thing in the first studies is to train obedience between the sense of hearing and the free adjustment of the producing organs.

We often hear complaints as to the tongue being "too big" or "in the way." These sayings are nonsense; the tongue fits the mouth, rests in the lower jaw and the tip of the tongue, under natural and normal conditions, rests against the lower teeth without pressure.

Aside from the described production of vowels, I would like to mention their qualities as advantages or disadvantages.

Bright vowels help to thin the adjustment of our vocal chords and consequently aid, if properly produced, in brilliancy.

Dark vowels have a tendency to thicken and reduce the brilliancy of the vocal chord vibrations and consequently have a strong tendency to waste breath and produce the voice with a dull quality.

Therefore, in order to obtain the most advantageous

results in our work, we should as nearly as possible in our study of technique, alternate between bright, neutral and dark vowels. Thus the influence of each would be modified and the result would be normality. The knowledge of how to change the vowels as we practice is of the greatest benefit and should be taught to the pupil as soon as possible, because it trains him to think and to use his judgment and eventually to become his own master. Besides, the vowel forms are international, and we need something in our art that is tangible and indisputable in order to establish perfect diction in foreign languages.

Students who have difficulty in singing bright vowels in the upper voice, $\bar{e}$ and $\bar{\imath}$ for instance, or those who can not articulate $\bar{o}$ and $\overline{oo}$ in the high voice with brilliancy, are very deficient in technique and in sore need of true knowledge. They constantly cheat themselves by making compromises in their pronunciation and also do wrong in changing text to suit their inferior technique. If such students find no help in their teachers, there must be a lack of understanding on one side or the other.

In describing vowels the terms most generally used are "bright" and "dark," though sometimes they are compared to colors. There is no objection to such comparisons, but I use vowel construction as a basis of vocal training, and in order to make analytical work more clear I prefer an analysis in reference to form rather than color. Vowels are produced by different formations of the vocal tube and different positions of the epiglottis and lips. Consequently I classify the vowels for practical work as follows:

1. Broad or wide vowels (may also be called "bright"), $\bar{e} — \bar{a} — \breve{e}$.
2. Neutral vowels (may also be called "normal"), $a — (ah)$.
3. Elongated vowels (may also be called "dark" $a — (aw)$, $o — (oh)$, $oo — (boot)$.

4. Composite vowels (not used in English), ö — ü.

Broad vowels are formed by a tongue which is high and broad at the back; $\bar{e}$ the highest; ă and ĕ the lowest, but still with convex tongue.

The neutral vowel a (ah) (Italian) requires a low-grooved tongue and an arching of the soft palate.

In elongated vowels, $\overline{oo}$, the longest and also darkest, requires a lower larynx and consequently the root of the tongue and protruded lips.

Composite vowels, ö and ü, are combinations of the lip positions of $\bar{o}$ and $\overline{oo}$ and of the tongue positions of a and e, as will be shown in the table of vowels.

Elongation of the vocal tube means that the larynx lowers and that the lips protrude, the most important of which, however, is the lowering of the larynx. If the protrusion of the lips is overdone it gives the voice a hooting quality, dark and monotonous, and destroys charm and simplicity.

The following table of vowels in the Italian and English languages will help to elucidate my classification, and unquestionable benefit will be derived from a sufficient concentration on these examples.

1. Broad Vowels.
    English — ee (bee, see).
    Italian — i (vino; as English e in be).
    English — e (set, net).
    Italian — e (essere, febbre).
    English — a (day, ape).
    Italian — e (seno; as English a in fame).

2. Neutral Vowels.
    English — a (art, father).
    English — a (that, mat, cat).
    Italian — a (Alma, Madre; as English a in art).

3. Elongated Vowels.
English — a (awe, all, call).
English — o (blow, go, so).
Italian — o (poverta, amore; as English o in note).
English — oo (boot, cool).
Italian — u (fuggire, sventura, cuba; as English oo in coo).
4. Composite Vowels.
German — o (schön, söhne).
French — o (peu).
German — u (süss, Grüsse).
French — u (Rue, perdue).

It is most important for the student while singing not to think of the letters, but of the vowel as *sound* and *form* united. The exercises given are so constructed as to promote facility in thinking as well as in production.

The bright vowels, $\bar{e}$, $\breve{e}$ and $\bar{a}$, have a strong tendency to close the vocal lips and make them vibrant. This is advantageous; but is attended by the danger of raising the larynx too high, on account of the high tongue, and, if this be overdone, it can lead to pressure. It is therefore incumbent, when studying bright vowels, that we use a soft throat, loose larynx, a very relaxed tongue, with as much broad space in the back as possible. Our hearing gives us the power to control these bright vowels so that they neither become dark, covered nor thick, and are not produced with greater resistance or nasal resonance than the other vowels. The elongated vowels have a tendency to lessen or slacken the vibratory qualities of the vocal chords and at the same time possess the advantages of a darker color and a lower larynx. Properly produced, the neutral vowel *a* (*ah*) (Italian) should have the good qualities of both the broad and elongated vowels which may be called width and depth.

The knowledge of the various vowel combinations, according to the nature of the particular organ, enables the student to surmount many difficulties and is so valuable and important in the singing of exercises and text that it opens up new possibilities to those possessing the knowledge. One of the most important effects is that it enables the singer to pronounce with such freedom that the smallest tone-color or nuance will find expression. In the absence of such knowledge, physical effort must be resorted to for producing the desired effects. Singers who open the mouth after each syllable waste a considerable amount of energy without any beneficial result — for it should be borne in mind that the finest diction is not the most visible.

Exercise in front of a mirror and try to attain perfect pronunciation with as little facial movement as possible.

Consonants

Consonants. From the above we have seen that vowels depend upon the form of the vocal tube and the position of the epiglottis and, to a certain extent, upon the tensity of the vocal lips or chords. Consonants, however, are produced through an interference to the continued flow of tone. This interference occurs in three places within the vocal tube which I shall call points of articulation.

1. Through the lips or between the lower lip and the upper teeth.
2. Between the tip of the tongue and the upper teeth.
3. Between the back of the tongue and the soft palate.

Consonants are also practically classified as:

Explosive — sounding and explosive.
Hissing — hissing and sounding.
Trembling — R- lip R, tongue R, palate R.
Nasal — M, N.
Aspirated — H.

First position of articulation.	Second position of articulation.	Third position of articulation.
Explosive–Explo. & Sound.	Explosive–Explo. & Sound.	Explosive–Explo. & Sound.
P B	T D	K G
Hissing– Hissing & Sound	Hissing– Hissing & Sound	Hissing– Hissing & Sound.
F V	S Z	Sch Dj
	Sounding L	
	Tongue — used R	Palate — used R
Sounding Nasal M	Sounding N	Sounding Ng

Aspirant — H produced in the larynx — (*ha*).

The Vowel — E

English speaking singers, especially women, experience difficulty in producing the bright vowels pure in the upper part of the voice.

The trouble is so general, that many teachers make compromises as to their production in the pure form, and even books have been written advising students against their use.

It would be better to advise the student to seek technical knowledge that would conquer these difficulties. I believe that anyone upon reflection would see the absurdity of acknowledging the impossibility of producing the vowels of our language in singing, especially when singers of the Italian nation sing these vowels with the greatest facility and with clear, beautiful, free tones.

The cause of this difficulty in English-speaking singers

PLATE 8

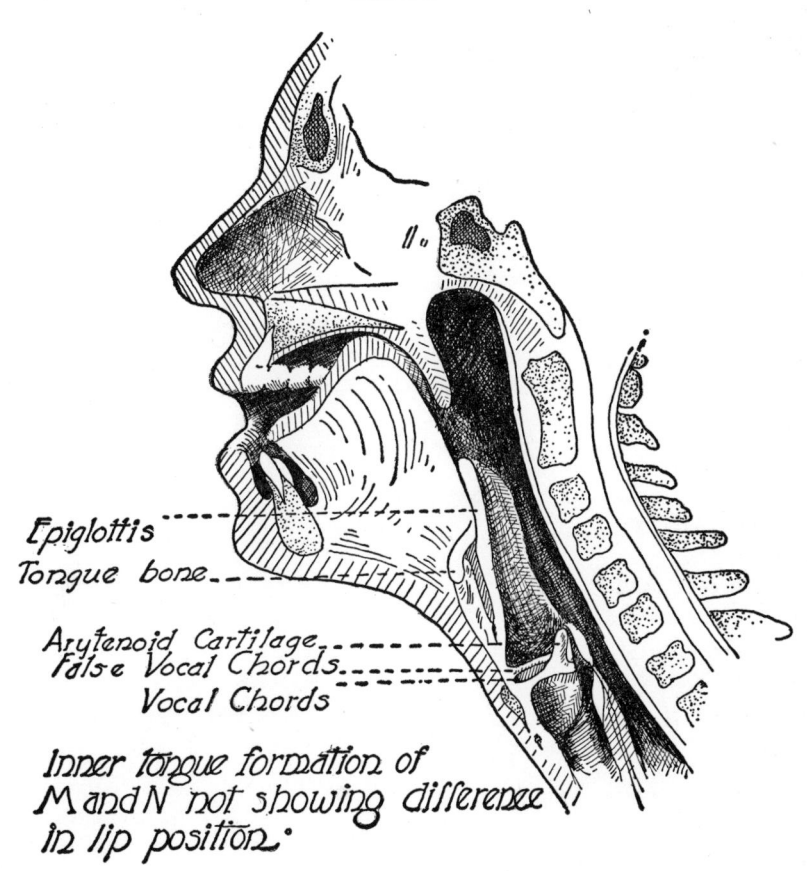

Epiglottis
Tongue bone
Arytenoid Cartilage
False Vocal Chords
Vocal Chords

Inner tongue formation of M and N not showing difference in lip position.

is the habit, formed usually in childhood, of producing the bright vowels in low nose resonance instead of head resonance. It has been mentioned in other chapters on vowel construction that the epiglottis must stand perpendicular

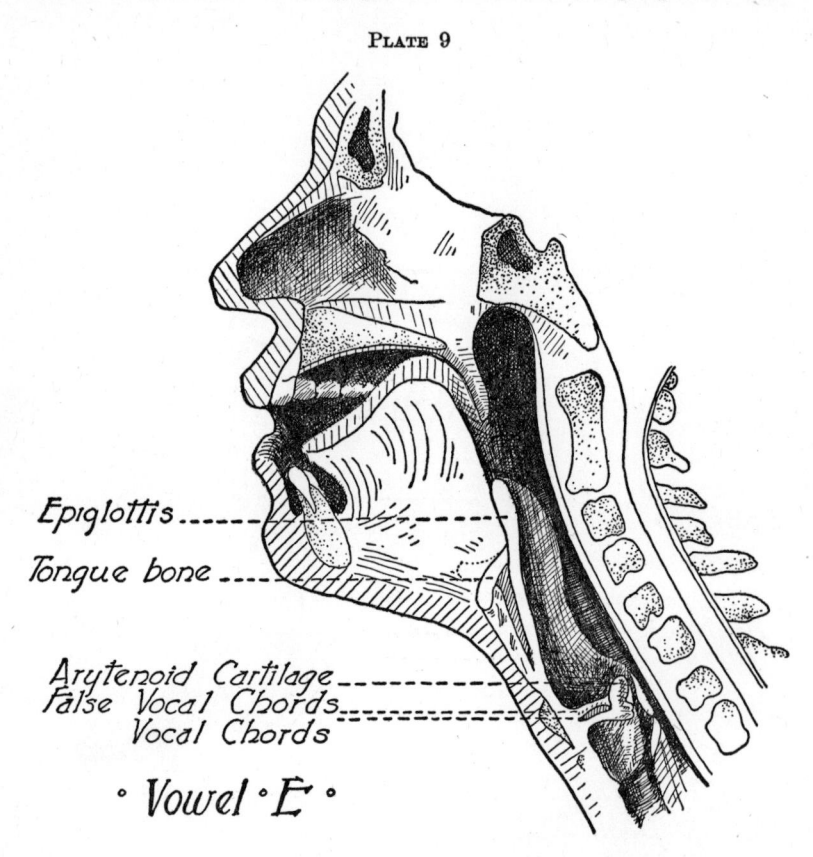

PLATE 9

Epiglottis
Tongue bone
Arytenoid Cartilage
False Vocal Chords
Vocal Chords

° Vowel ° E °

for the bright vowels and as this cannot be accomplished with a low grooved tongue, it is necessary to arch the tongue high in the back for the bright vowels rather than to drop the arching of the palate. If the arching of the veils of the **palate drops, the sound enters the nasal cavity and loses** its freedom of head resonance and becomes forced and pinched. I advise students who are deficient on this point to articulate *ah — oh — ee,* one after the other, and feel the same resonance on last vowels as on the first ones,

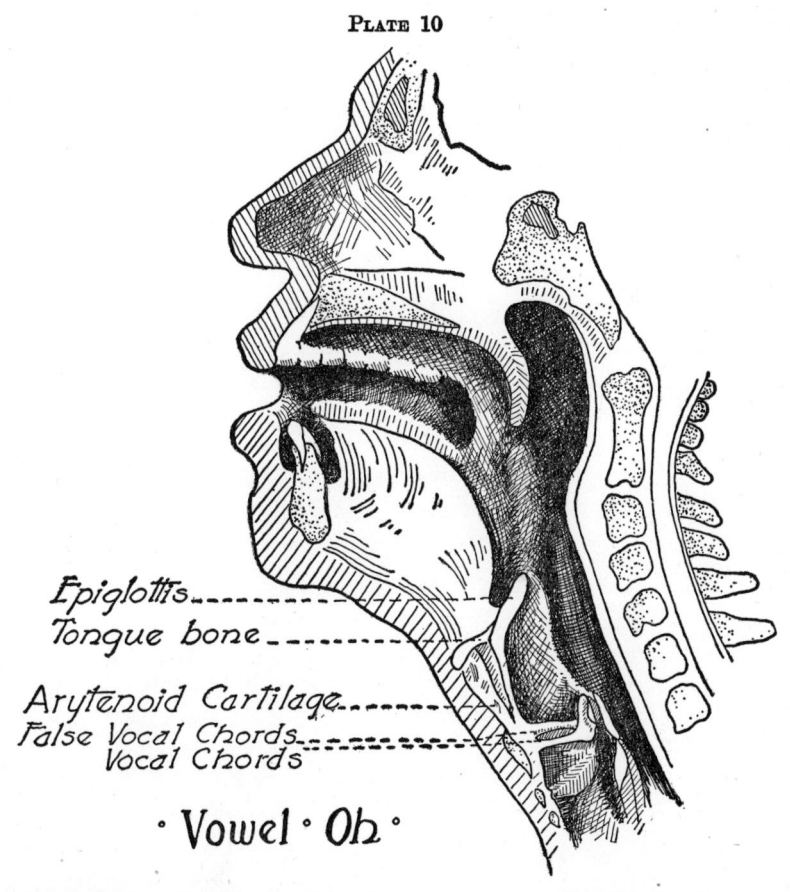

PLATE 10

Epiglottis
Tongue bone
Arytenoid Cartilage
False Vocal Chords
Vocal Chords

· Vowel · Oh ·

not being afraid to raise the tongue in the back for the vowel *ee.* After this becomes natural and comfortable, proceed to sing small scales, on all three vowels, taking great care that the singing of the vowel *ee* does not change to a nasal resonance, feeling it in the same place of production as *ah* and *oh*, rather back of the root of the tongue, and very broad; but prevent it from suddenly changing into a sound more nasal than *ah* and *oh*. This difficulty, however, usually disappears by itself when the student learns to hear the difference between head and nasal resonance and by changing on all the different vowel combinations indicated in our exercises, the bright vowels soon become as free and comfortable as neutral and dark vowels.

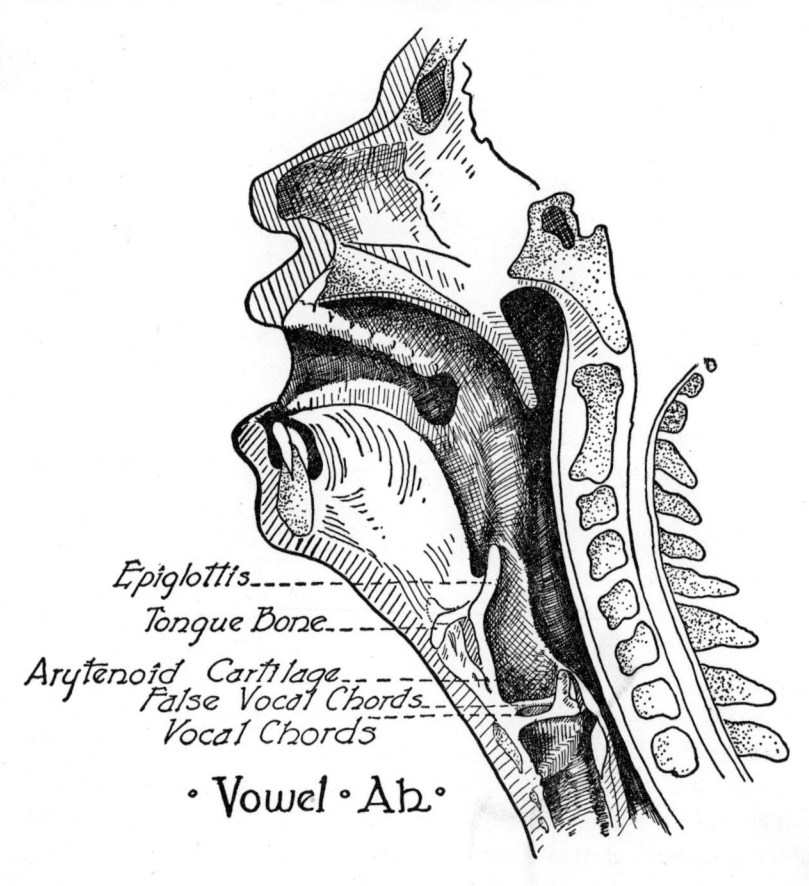

° Vowel ° Ah °

CHAPTER X
Articulation

By *articulation* we mean the vocal utterance of words, their consonants as well as their vowels. These words make up our text. Not considering the treatment of text from its dramatic or musical side, I wish to make some remarks that are based on many years experience.

From the description of vowels and consonants we see that the flow of the voice is on the vowel and that the consonant is comparatively without head-resonance, in fact is an obstacle. If we attempt to place the vowel as the consonant is placed, then the resonance of the vowel suffers. On the other hand, if we let our consonants fall or become weak, our text becomes insipid.

Many singers in an attempt to create a fine *legato* overdo the blending of these two sound-formations (vowels and consonants) and the result is a lack of distinctness; if they dwell too long on the consonants, lack of carrying power, — in fact, a diminishing of the size of the voice. This misuse of articulation is very dangerous and deceptive and ends almost always in pressure on the voice.

When, on the contrary, the singer gives to his consonants the necessary energy required by their musical and dramatic accent, and then goes over on the vowel as soon as possible, letting the tip of the tongue assume its natural position against the roots of the lower front teeth after the giving of the consonant, the voice then gains in carrying power and tone-color.

In reality, by holding vowels and consonants in their respective places we give the most carrying power to the tone as well as distinctness of diction.

I ask my readers to think over these words and experiment from an objective standpoint. I have seen many sad cases where lovely big voices have become dull and pressed through a false comprehension of articulation. When the same singers were taught a proper understanding of articulation their voices became free and beautiful to an unbelievable extent. The consonants are the contours in the text-picture, the rhythm and accent; but the tone-color, volume and shading belong to the vowels.

Normal Voice

Each individual singer, vocalizing correctly, has an individual normal voice quality, a quality as characteristic as the individual's physiognomy. This normality is lost when the singer is wrongly trained. When, for instance, his voice is being trained darker or whiter or bigger or higher than Nature's intention, the result is inevitably a confused mental state regarding the use of his voice. How often we hear voices so distorted that we hardly recognize any natural qualities; the training has been detrimental instead of beneficial.

It is not to be understood, however, that all good natural voices are perfect. The terms *natural* and *normal* in regard to the voice are not the same. A voice for different reasons may *naturally* be over-nasal, over-dark, over-white, breathy or dull; but once these flaws are corrected, it approaches *normality* and the singer finds the tone-quality which gives the greatest freedom in producing all vowels, different volumes and tone-heights, with comfort, beauty and durability.

Thus we grow from the natural to the normal, and further, to the ideal which is umlimited in growth as long as the singer devotes his mental powers to rendering his songs as nearly as possible in harmony with the conception of the poet and composer.

The normal voice, if distorted through wrong training, cannot be restored in any way other than through the sense of hearing. The first definite step is to learn to hear vowels *pure*, — to recognize their definite forms, aside from the numerous nuances of tone-color which the vowels assume in words under different conditions of expression.

The ability to discern the pure vowel form is sadly neglected by singers of other than the Latin race. The Italian, for instance, has the keenest ear for perfect vowels and consequently the keenest ear for perfect tones. This is a result of the throat instinctively obeying the perfect ear. We find more correct singing among the Italians than among the people of any other nation. Especially is their normal tone-color more frequently found unimpaired. This is a result of their language. This superiority is often noted in close comparison between Italian singers and singers of other nationalities; and although the latter sometimes equal the Italians, they never *excel* them.

The principle upon which is based the training that enables the singer to recognize the normal quality of his own voice will be described later in another chapter.

Perhaps it would be well to draw a comparison in order to make it still clearer regarding the individual normal tone-color and its value as recognized by the artist. Take for instance, two well-known tenors, Bonci and the lamented Caruso, both indisputable artists, singing the same role, *Rudolph* in " La Boheme," each in his own most favorable tone-color. Caruso singing the above role with the tone-color of Bonci, which would mean Bonci's normal voice color, would have seemed absurd; Bonci using the so characteristic normal tone-color of Caruso would be equally absurd. This example is to show that each artist must find the tone-color which best represents his most comfortable and durable voice and which I call his "normal voice."

Low Medium C to G

Few singers realize the value of understanding this interval of the voice and most peculiar and interesting it is, this fifth from C to G, whatever the nature of the voice, high or low, male or female. The difficulty in recognizing this fifth lies in the fact that when used wrongly, it does not sound badly enough to be recognized as wrong by some teachers and singers. This part of the voice represents the usual range of the speaking voice, as nearly all speakers in languages not of Latin origin, neglect the singing quality in speech, augmenting the nasal tendency of the consonants and neglecting the singing head-resonance which usually we have to teach the pupil to hear. Of course, there are exceptional speakers who produce the English language beautifully in spoken voice, but they are rare. To return to the important fifth, I can best explain it thus: those placing this fifth in low, nose resonance are limited in making the voice ascend unless they change their adjustment. The consequence is resonance somewhere between B flat and E flat. Those placing this fifth in head-resonance instead of low nose or consonant resonance, can ascend without change, having naturally the fundamental principle of the one-register scale as their basis of technique; but an equally important reason for using this fifth with head-resonance is the difference in carrying quality — the voice thus produced being far more brilliant and never requiring extra pressure in production. It descends much further with clearness in the low voice, secures female voices against the use of the wrong chest voice, and enables the singer to reach with the top voice without change of quality and with no extra effort. This fifth is not easily produced, when the mouth positions are too open; in fact, it is dependent upon an arched inner mouth, arched veils of the palate, which prevent the vibratory air column from entering the nasal cavity, causing consonant resonance in overproportion. A certain amount of low nose-resonance exists in all tones, in fact, we could not produce a tone without it; but we have to learn to use the minimum low nose-resonance and the maximum head-resonance, sometimes called *post nasal* or high nose-resonance, a term I am opposed to, as it is misleading.

It is work for any student to concentrate his mind on this point of the fifth between C and G. I have frequently heard it called *mixed* voice, and if this helps my readers to find it, well and good; but I consider it as brilliant as the upper medium, with only slightly less volume under normal production.

Intonation

Perfect intonation is the product of the correct number of vibrations to a given period, for instance, a second. If the number be too great, the tone is sharp; too few, the tone is flat. The causes of these faults are the same in male and female voices.

I have described the two ways of producing tones; the right way, where the chords meet after each vibration, the wrong way, the falsetto or open glottis mode, which is the opposite of the other. Women, also tenors, who make use of the falsetto are apt to sing sharp in the top register. For example, when singers, in practice while learning roles or new music, sing with open glottis or with falsetto instead of with a perfectly placed small voice. The chords through which an unnecessarily large volume of air passes, by reason of the open or badly closed glottis, produce an increased number of vibrations which gives the tone a "hooting" color very similar to the sound of wind blowing through a chimney. Then when volume is to be produced, the chords have no resistance and intonation becomes uncertain. Male and female singers who fall into the habit of breathy singing, lose the elasticity of the vocal lips and when volume is required are apt to sing off the key.

Singing off-key is not necessarily due to defective hearing, for many singers who do not hear when they themselves sing off-key, detect it at once when others do so. The cause is a wrong way of singing. If the ear were at fault all singing would be imperfect, not only certain tones. Voices which sound flat throughout fall short of overtones. This is often caused by fatigue or pressed diction or by singing higher than the nature of the voice. Nature has not provided us all with the same degree of aural perception, but *ear-training* can bring about much improvement in the hearing of intonation.

To correct intonation a proper adjustment of the closing of the glottis is imperative. The breath should be so controlled or balanced that it will not meet the vocal lips more heavily than is necessary, as breath forced against the chords impairs their ability to vibrate with sufficient elasticity, which is equivalent to pressing. As the first step in technical training, the vocal lips should be thinly adjusted, as the lack of such adjustment causes off-key singing.

Singers who have carried their thick voice too high or have pressed the top voice, find that when an attempt is made to remedy this fault, the chords do not intonate, having become weak and having lost their elasticity. This condition can produce paralysis of the chords for which the only sure cure is rest and the recommencement of study under most careful judgment.

In all these cases high singing, even though the **higher**

voice be surprisingly better than the medium or low, would only tend to keep the vocal lips from regaining their elasticity.

Singers aiming at nasal tone-placing also incur danger of singing off-key, as pressure must be brought to bear on the vibratory organs in order to produce volume, the nasal resonance being dull compared to skull or head-resonance. Singers who do not use nasal tones have more head or skull resonance. Also, pressing on consonants causes weak intonation, as consonants have more dull resonance and are wanting in skull or head resonance.

Thus we see that our main object must be to obtain a balance of adjustment in the attack of the tone. If we exert pressure similar to the pressure of those using the stroke of the glottis, we thicken the chords, which prevents them from vibrating with sufficient rapidity and elasticity. All these errors can only be overcome when breath-form is free and normal, as the closing of the vocal lips bears automatic relationship to the breath. If we feel the necessity of gripping or pinching in the attack, it is wrong and forced; in a balanced attack we feel a natural ease in our throat.

The perfect manner of attacking a tone is not to permit a small amount of breath to escape through the glottis before issuing the tone, but on the contrary, to allow a very small hesitation of the breath before issuing the tone. But this latter is not to be falsely understood as an exaggerated stroke of the glottis, — a gentle attack of the glottis is the proper attack.

Singers who, beginning with correct intonation, find themselves gradually going off the key, or whose sustained tone gradually darkens, are singing with a too thick adjustment of the vocal chords. The breath, being insufficient to keep the vocal lips vibrating, cannot sustain true intonation. Singers who favor over-dark tones as a standard tone-color are apt to exaggerate, which leads to off-key singing.

From the foregoing we may conclude that as all musical instruments have facilities for increasing the number of vibrations, so, as the vibratory organs become shorter and thinner, the tone becomes higher; and whereas the human voice depends upon only one set of chords and for this reason must adjust the length and thickness of these for every tone, so is it imperative that the ability of the adjustment of these vocal chords be not impaired or abused. We cannot in a stringed instrument bring a string above a certain tension for which it is intended without its eventually breaking. The same is the case with the voice when it is over-adjusted or over-tightened.

Correct adjustment becomes instinctive and also subconscious as the hearing of the student is being trained regarding the judging of cause and effect.

The most common fault is that of forcing or pressing. It appears in different ways and has different causes, usually the lack of good fundamental study. This evil most frequently appears as a throaty quality of the voice or a nasal twang or a *tremolo*.

To sing without forcing means that the voice is so balanced in its production that it yields the maximum results with the minimum effort. This point of perfection can be arrived at only when the artist thoroughly understands his normal voice as well as normal breathing.

The first fault, throaty singing, is a result of a forced larynx position or of tongue pressure on the epiglottis, which prevents its freedom for vowel production, and becomes an obstacle to the sound-waves. This error alone prevents free diction; and many other faults naturally arise from this evil.

Nasal singing, or nasal twang, is easily felt when we pinch our nostrils. Once overcome in exercises, care must be taken that the error does not reappear when singing text.

It requires a very keen ear to detect this fault in the low and medium voices when the fault is not present in marked degree.

Tremolo, perhaps the most discouraging fault of all, is a result of various causes, usually an unsteady diaphragm, caused by wrong breathing; or, it may be the result of a wrong larynx position. This latter result is caused by lack of vowel variety in exercises, or, better said, by training the larynx too high in general. When the *tremolo* is a result of yelling in the top voice or screaming too high, the fault is very difficult to remedy; at times perfect rest and a new beginning prove beneficial; but the new work must be done with utmost care.

For the overcoming of the first fault, throaty singing, I know of no better cure than to sing with as little effort as possible on all the different vowels in one breath, taking care that no vowel assumes more pressure or less resonance than any other vowel. In this work both high and low range must be excluded. Devices like a triangular piece of wood to be placed between the teeth to hold down the tongue, or a teaspoon to press it down, are, to my mind, useless. The moment the obstacle is removed, the tongue jumps up high. We must also remember that high as well as low tongue positions are necessary for the production of vowels.

For overcoming nasal twang I have no better advice to give than the foregoing.

For the overcoming of *tremolo*, no matter what the cause, I believe in the thorough reviewing of all technical work; first of all, freedom of vowel production, and next, understanding of breath-form. I must here again emphasize the necessity of understanding that different tone-heights and different tone-sizes correctly produced without forcing are not dependent upon different breath pressures. The more we relax our abdomen when inhaling, the more ease and energy we have when exhaling and this energy never becomes forced. On the contrary, if we create energy necessary for the tone-production by drawing or pressing on a badly inhaled breath-form, the tone becomes forced, usually throaty and unsteady.

While working against *tremolo* it is a mistake to sing only sustained voice. On the contrary, start an exercise rather fast and then let the voice on the same breath reduce the pace to a slow tempo. Do not repeat the exercises in the chromatic following keys, but change in the intervals according to the scale. For instance, a scale of four tones: first, key of C, then F, then C♯, then F♯, and so on. But in all cases patience and will-power are great factors in overcoming the faults of unsteadiness of the voice, or *tremolo*.

Many other faults such as slurring up to the tones, pressing on consonants, over-accentuating end-syllables are all faults which can be overcome by honest and repeated criticism.

The causes of singing flat and sharp have been described in separate chapters and need not be mentioned further here.

Throaty or Guttural

A teacher may say to a pupil when a tone is wrongly produced, "That is throaty. Sing without your throat." Our good teacher means well; perhaps is sufficiently ignorant to think that we can sing without our throats and, in covering up his ignorance by false suggestions, harms the growth of the pupil by keeping logic out of his mind. It is as logical to tell the vocal student to sing without his throat as it is to tell the violin student to play without strings. I have heard people, students and teachers, in their profound ignorance point out the most wonderful self-invented methods of singing in which the throat has absolutely nothing to do with it. Of course this type of teacher belongs at best to the blind leading the blind. The real meaning of the criticism "throaty singing," is that the throat is being wrongly used. A man says, "I have a temperature." He means that he has a fever, an abnormal condition of temperature. So in singing, "throaty" means an abnormal condition of the throat.

As we have seen, the larynx and the vocal chords are the all-important parts of the singing instrument, and a knowledge of their functions is of the utmost importance to singers. Through such understanding and the training of the sense of hearing, the throat becomes obedient and performs like second nature,—a most ideal condition for vocalists.

Covering

Covering is a term used, I daresay, by all students and teachers. Its meaning is vague to the beginner.

The average vocal teacher does not pay sufficient attention to the low or medium voice, and in ascending scales the voice reaches a place, somewhere around B flat to E, where it seems to be in need of a change in production before it can proceed upward. The usual remedy is to change the vowel in its form to a darker vowel This subterfuge is *covering;* and is recommended for example, in methods which teach the pupil never to sing the Italian *A* (*Ah*) above *C* sharp, but to change it to *Aw*. This and other compromises come from lack of real knowledge.

If we use the term *covering*, it is only because we are forced to do so, as it has become a common vocal term. But perfect singing has no one-place covering. The one-register scale properly executed on pure vowels, the larynx placed with freedom and no pressure to resist, would produce the voice absolutely and perfectly rounded in tone-color. With increasing brilliancy and warmth of tone, we must allow our voice to ascend automatically, keeping the arched veils of the palate generously high; then the voice assumes the quality of rounded, increased head-resonance without pressure, thus preventing a blatant quality.

The middle voice wrongly produced will lead us into trouble. These troubles arise first of all when in any voice, whether the bass or the highest soprano, the tones between C and G, lower medium, are wrongly produced. These tones do not definitely *sound* nor *feel* badly if produced with low nose resonance, or perhaps minimum head-resonance would be more accurate. These tones, when wrongly resonated, thicken the vocal chords. Here, in saying "wrongly resonated" I do not speak of the common error of *diffusion*. I speak only of *wrong resonating*. The wrong resonance in the low and low-medium, the tone short of head-resonance, thickens the vocal chords which in return demand extra energy to produce volume. This extra energy soon turns into pressure, the beginning of forcing; and reaching anywhere from B flat to F sharp, according to the range, the voice needs suddenly to change in its production owing to a change of quality. In some voices, more frequently in men's voices, this quality is a hard, pressed tone, and in women's voices, a weaker diffused tone that is apt to be very pointed if attempt is made to put such a tone over into *forte*. It is very difficult for such voices to pronounce vowels purely between D and G, high medium.

Covering is caused by a succession of tones badly balanced which then need readjustment for progression. If we balance our E flat, for example, in the low medium voice, so that, without change of quality, it will ascend or descend five tones with ease on all vowels, we have laid a fine foundation for the balancing of our entire voice. At the same time we train the ear to recognize the smallest nuances in tone-color without any fatigue to the voice. The principle that makes the low and medium voices join and equalize is the same that joins the medium and high voices, each tone so balanced that it ascends and descends without change in production and consequently no change in quality. It is here to be emphasized that the one-register scale is the result of distributing or balancing the so-called register difficulties over the entire range of the voice.

Open Singing

By *open singing* is meant singing that is lacking in color, especially dark color, which results from the exaggerated opening of the throat. It is an ugly, common quality, lacking in nobility, and approaches "screaming" in its blatancy.

Open singing is frequently heard in vaudeville, and among Italian street-singers.

This open voice quality should by all means be kept out of the training of any singer aiming at a noble art. The *buffo* singer, however, must at times apply this tone-color to express ignoble sentiments. But these branches of the art of singing take care of themselves or can only be treated as special cases.

The too *white* singing, analyzed from a physical viewpoint, is a result of a too high larynx, too much low-spreading of the veils of the palate and a thin adjustment of the vocal chords. The matter of adjustment often misleads singers into taking their high tones too open and white in order to facilitate production. This is a great error, as we can adjust our vocal chords thinly without the necessity of singing open or white. The noble tone-color is a result of thin vocal chord adjustment giving brilliancy and a low larynx giving dark and warm color. It is to be remembered that the lowering of the larynx need not make the vocal tube narrow, in which case the tone-color would only be darkened and would lack in warmth and brilliancy. The noble tone is a combination of width and depth in adjustment and warmth and brilliance in result.

Somber Timbre

The term *timbre* is used here to express the quality of color in the voice.

Somber timbre is the result of a lowering of the larynx and of the veils of the palate. It is an absolutely legitimate tone-color frequently demanded and most valuable in expressing certain moods. But somber *timbre* must not be the habitual tone-color produced, as this would eventually lead the voice into the pitiful condition of volume without brilliancy, — a most monotonous, tedious production which results in singing off-key.

Close and somber *timbres* are secondary tone-colors, not fundamentals.

Warning must be given the student who thinks that close and somber *timbres* add volume to a voice. To the contrary, the carrying power of the voice if produced too somber is greatly impaired.

The drawing up of the uvula lowers the veils of the palate and consequently makes the tone-color somber. Great care must be used on this point, as voices thus produced soon become, in a general way, strange and instrumental in sound and find great difficulty in producing pure vowels. Female voices trained to raise the uvula instead of arching the veils of the palate, frequently get a secondary sound similar to a harmonica. In male voices this method has a tendency to diminish the natural volume of the top voice.

Bright Timbre

When the vocal chords vibrate thinly, which is a result of true balance and no over-burdened breath, the vibrations are clear and in return, the resonance is clear.

The physical conditions producing bright *timbre* have as a basis of direction a predominating feeling of width. We sense our bright vowels, *e, i, a, ĕ,* broader in their production than the darker vowels *oo, o, a*. Consequently the augmented width of our vocal tube while producing the tone would be instrumental in intensifying the brighter vocal *timbre*. If, however, this is exaggerated, for instance, by vocal practice on all bright vowels, there would be a danger of singing too white or blatant. This is frequently heard in methods miscalled Italian methods, but which, in reality, bear no relation to the noble art that has come from Italian singers. The Italian method, if we recognize a method as such, could only be one that beautifies, enriches, and, above all, gives nobility and authority to the voice. These qualities all disappear where voices are trained too bright without depth of tone-color.

Singing Forward

The term, *singing forward*, so frequently used, is a most misleading one. We sing neither forward, backward, upward nor downward. These terms of direction when used regarding tone can only be suggestive of some deficiency or extreme quality of the tone. Usually the term for placing the voice forward merely stands equivalent to good singing; but no more than that. The head-resonance that makes the voice perfect is a result of proper balance, but not of placing the voice, as is so often and misleadingly said, in the mask of the face. Here we find the consonant part of the voice, but not the vowel part that constitutes the floating resonance.

Feeling the resonance in the mask of the face indicates only good; but it is not a principle upon which we can base a method.

Make perfect the *cause*, and perfect *results* will follow. Ignorance of causes makes all attempts to correct faults a dangerous business.

One reason that a free tone is felt in the mask is that the nerves in the mask of the face are so very sensitive that we feel more there than in the back part of the skull. Scientifically tested, the resonances of the skull are stronger than those of the mask of the face.

Diffused Singing

Diffused singing is a common fault, so common that the Italians think that most foreigners, especially those speaking English, sing without brilliancy; that their singing is *diffused*. Comparatively speaking, diffused singing would correspond to a liquid diluted; the substance reduced in its natural intensity.

In diffused singing the air exhaled is not entirely converted into clear resonance and lacks some of its natural brilliancy. The extreme of diffused singing is breathy singing. We often find this diffusion where the singer has forced, and in trying to soften his voice in order to overcome forcing, loses the brilliancy. At other times we have singers who diffuse their voices in *pianissimo*. Barytones, especially, in their *mezza voce*, are liable to this defect, which is dangerous when the voice is obliged to produce big brilliant tones; it loses its ability to produce a real climax. Also, voices that sing an over-amount of dark vowels in practice, are apt to sing diffused.

The disadvantages of diffused singing are the following: lack of brilliancy; waste of breath; great fatigue where *forte* is demanded; lack of absolute carrying power; and a very indistinct pronunciation in the upper medium voice.

The cure of this fault is to learn to hear the difference between brilliant and dull singing and forced resonance. While the voice is using too much breath between C and E for high voices, and between A and C for low voices, the fault is not overcome. It cannot be cured by pressing with the breath nor by raising the chest; these latter remedies could only help very temporarily. Diffused singing is best overcome by a perfect balance of breath without forcing and this naturally needs the keenest judgment and sense of hearing on the part of both pupil and teacher. Often the application of *parlando* pronunciation in the medium voice points out the error most clearly to the student.

Humming

The reasons why *humming* is misleading and, in many cases harmful, are not difficult to explain if my readers will listen to logic.

By humming, we understand singing with the mouth closed, the voice being produced only through the nasal cavity. Observe a skull and notice what little opportunity there is of making the skull reverberate or resound through the nasal cavity compared with the back part of the skull which is supported by the vertebrae. Observe that with the mouth closed, articulation of vowels is impossible. Notice that the sound obtained while humming, is identical to that of a consonant. Observe that consonants are very inferior in resonance to vowels, consequently a vowel partly or almost entirely placed in the position of that taken by the humming voice, could only lose in resonance and never gain. The tone-waves leaving the open mouth give our vowels their form. If any of these tone-waves or vibrations are unnecessarily directed into the nasal cavity, the distinctness of our vowel is lessened. The effort of the singer to produce volume in the nasal cavity, which is dull by nature, could only eventually teach him to force. Consequently, all humming, if done for the purpose of placing the voice perfectly, is contradictory to the laws of singing laid down by nature.

Exercises coupling vowels with nasal consonants are, at best, bad, if the aim is to place vowels where the consonants are felt. Exercises producing vowels and consonants coupled, keeping the consonants distinct consonants and the vowels brilliant in head-resonance, *legato* or unbroken, are, of course, beneficial. But the usual humming exercises where M and N are rapidly repeated are meaningless and a detriment to the vowel resonance. I daresay, whatever, if any, good is obtained through these different humming methods, is not due to the humming and could be learned in other more simple and more logical ways which coincide with Nature's intentions.

Head Voice

Much has been said on this subject by writers on the Art of Singing. *Head voice* is in reality only a term, often used in a very misleading manner. In order that we may think for ourselves, let us remember that all tones are produced in the larynx and that all resonance is a reverberation or resounding of the head or skull.

Different modes of producing vibration cause different kinds of resonance. The vibrations based on the principle of a perfect closure of the glottis between each two vibrations, result in a different character of resonance from the tones produced with a less perfect closure of the glottis (diffused). Or when the glottis remains slightly open (falsetto), the tone takes on a flute-like quality; if extremely open, a hooting quality.

Looking at our resonating organs. There are two, opening at the upper pharynx; one into the nasal cavity, Nature's provision for nasal consonants; and one blocking the nasal cavity by raising the veils of the palate, thus obtaining vowel resonance. In this latter the head-resonance is very clear and brilliant if properly produced.

It is to be remembered that the resonances are produced only through transmission by the vertebrae, the vibrating air-column and the inner walls of the vocal tube; the latter delicate and movable and able to mold certain forms that correspond to our vowels. This is the extent of our affirmative knowledge of how to produce head-resonance. It is best produced by not overburdening the vibrating organs with breath pressure which puts the throat in a stiff position, gradually lowers the veils of the palate and directs the vibrating air-column against the hard-palate. This is one of the greatest dangers in singing as it destroys the freedom of the tone and gives the voice a most characterless, pinched, sickly quality and interferes with the development of volume in the upper range of the voice.

Again I must warn the student against nasal singing if in search of head-resonance or head voice. Those very high tones so rarely heard, that float and are extremely rich in head-resonance without forcing, are results of what the Italians call an "open throat." In fact, the Italians say, "Open the throat, and the result is head voice." This can be true enough for the Italians; but if exaggerated by singers of other nations, it would, in many cases, give the voice a strange secondary quality that obviously would detract from the normal voice quality.

Singers who have facility for this kind of extremely heady tone production should never neglect mixing this tone with a certain amount of *parlando* quality, as it helps the tone in uniting with the more substantial voice quality, and will help them to get the so-called " head voice " so united with the normal tone quality that the voice will go over on big *forte* tones. We seldom hear this, but it can be done. I feel that it should not be attempted until all vocal conditions are perfect, when the judgment of the tone-color and vowel form is under control. I have had the most unexpected results in the production of the so-called " head-tone " in the upper voice, but only through indirect training and through the influence of vowel-form to place the larynx and mold of the vocal tube in a position to produce these head tones, or intense head resonance, with security and perfect vowel-form. The head tone which does not permit pronunciation nor *crescendo* is imperfect and misleading and best left alone; it can cause great confusion in the singer's sense of hearing his own voice.

The Vibrating Air-Column

The vibrating air-column is a splendid term and most expressive of the actual existing condition of the vocal organs in the act of singing. It is a term frequently mentioned by writers of singing methods. Some have reference to the vibrating air-column including the concentrated air in the windpipe and lungs. This is by no means a bad thought but is misleading because the air-column does not vibrate until the vocal chords convert it into a vibrating air-column. The reason I like the word " column " is because it gives me the idea of something plastic and perpendicular in direction; and that is the correct thought, because the vocal tube which gives form to this air-column is mostly perpendicular. And, in singing a tone, I like the sensation which I feel of the head or skull resting and resounding upon this air-column with freedom; but this latter impression is my individual fancy, not a fact, and belongs to what I call "my personal and own individual feeling of the tone."

But if we say, as I have often heard, "Direct the vibrating air-column against the teeth" or "hard-palate" or "cavities in the forehead," I feel danger of the suggestion being misleading, because the moment we "direct" this air-column we must change the form of the vocal tube and it at once loses its feeling of freedom and in most cases the voice becomes forced. The thought of directing against one place robs the voice of that perfect free, resonating quality which is most important to any voice, and is often called the "floating quality" and justly so, because it is not directed against anything nor held — it *floats*. Practically speaking, I daresay that the method of training voices to direct this vibrating air-column against the hard-palate usually leads to forcing and destroys the floating, free resonance and makes the pronunciation of certain vowels almost impossible.

It is, however, to be remembered that when we do not direct the vibrating air-column to any certain point but rather feel it filling every space within our heads with perfect free resonance, then we also feel that the hard-palate, even the teeth, reverberate. This sensation is a good sign, indicating freedom. But if we try to obtain this vibration of the hard-palate by directing against it, we are apt to go astray. The vibration of the hard-palate is a result, not a cause, and it must be recognized only as such.

Tenor-Barytone

From time to time attempts have been made to raise barytone voices to tenor voices. In some cases a certain amount of success has followed, artistic as well as financial, especially where the voices were marvelous in quality. But to the sincere and honest critic the question was always open as to the voice being a "made" tenor or a "natural" tenor. In all cases the lives of such voices have been short and uncertain, attended by too much transposed singing; and when the born tenor appeared, the difference was always too marked. I think that those who heard the last singing of "Lohengrin" by such a voice, when almost the entire role was sung below pitch to a noticeable extent, felt the sad farewell of the voice of a great artist.

I had the opportunity in Berlin, to observe a most interesting case of this kind. At the Royal Opera a barytone of wonderful voice facility and phenomenal voice quality attempted the raising of his voice to that of a tenor. His first appearance as "Lohengrin" impressed those who had never heard him, but disappointed those who had heard him as a barytone. The charm of his voice was lost, the wonderful floating quality which so marked his former singing was lost. This voice became, within one year, dull, nasal, forced and too low in intonation the moment he attempted higher roles. And this result is very frequent among singers less known. A voice refuses to be treated in a way different from that of its real natural tendency, and this should be a warning to young singers against believing all that *unscrupulous teachers promise*. It is safer to be a reliable high barytone than a forced-up, unreliable tenor. The method of pushing in the abdominal muscles in order to raise the chest high and force out high tones while the singer gets red in the face and the teacher talks "support," has done great harm in the world of singing students. Such voices become hard, unmusical and mechanical, uniform in size (and that usually a forced *forte*), frequently too low in intonation and always easily fatigued and husky in speaking voice after singing.

Perhaps mention should be made here that the above is true only of voices which are raised tenors or barytone-tenors, — naturally the tenor who was wrongly placed as a barytone finds relief when restored to his natural tenor *tessitura*.

The world's greatest barytone, Batistini, sang tenor for a short period, but soon realized his real voice and perhaps sings and has sung as perfectly as any living barytone of to-day. Those who have heard him sing the aria from " The Masked Ball " have truly something to remember in the way of perfect singing.

Laryngoscope Observations

Manuel Garcia, the inventor of the laryngoscope, proved through his invention that many a theory existing up to that time regarding voice phenomena was wrong. We should always be grateful to this great master for what he has taught us. He, who came from a family of the world's greatest singers and was himself a singer of great merit, a wonderful musician with an untiring mind and capacity for research, has in his work on the art of singing left us one of the most valuable, honest and sincere treatises on singing that exists. The Garcia Laryngoscope is being used to-day by almost all throat specialists, no change or improvements having been made since the original invention. The Garcia Laryngoscope has a disadvantage familiar to every one who has had his throat examined with it, namely, the discomfort that it causes while one produces a tone. In order to see the vocal chords one must sing a bright vowel, *i, e* or *e*. To do this the tongue must be high in the back to permit the epiglottis to stand high and not obstruct the view of the glottis, and this peculiar sensation of pronouncing with an open throat while having the desire to raise the tongue is not comfortable.

Later a laryngoscope was invented, a tubular instrument the thickness of a lead pencil, which, through the aid of prisms and lenses, reflects the picture of the inner throat, not reversed but normally. The light is obtained from a small but powerful electric lamp at the end of the instrument. This instrument is inserted along the side of the tongue, back to the rear wall of the throat, and a view can be obtained while the mouth is entirely closed.

To this instrument I have added an elbow at an obtuse angle and, through other combinations of prisms and lenses, I can see around the corner through this angle. Thus, I am able, while singing, to obtain a perfect picture of what happens in all ranges and powers of the voice. Also **I am** able to see the proportional changes in the glottis in the different ranges and the different positions for the epiglottis for the different vowels.

This instrument has enabled me to understand the entire mechanical part of the voice much more clearly than before, as I am now able to see, hear and feel the tone production at the same time. I do not mean to say that the use of an Auto Laryngoscope directly helps one to learn to sing, but it has enabled me to see with definite clearness many things that before were only theoretically known.

This instrument is registered in the German Patent Office as:—"*Auto Laryngoscope*" *nach Frantz Proschowsky D. B. G. M.*

CHAPTER XI
Study of Text

In studying text, the correct use of vowels and consonants is, naturally, of the utmost importance.

The consonants give the word its force, expressing the dramatic energy and activity of the underlying thought. The consonants beat time and give the rhythm decision.

The vowels, through their numerous colors and shadings, express the nature or sentiment of the song. Vowels have two accents:—first, the grammatical accent that falls on certain vowels in words; second, the emotional accent that either prolongs the tone, colors and intensifies it or, lastly, increases its height.

Music is written in regular, irregular and mixed time and the treatment of the same depends upon the singer's instinctive as well as his musical knowledge. This musical knowledge is absolutely necessary if real results are to be obtained.

Tone-production in itself expresses no decided idea. Melodies only awaken undecided feelings; still, in preparing text we must absolutely keep strictly to the music, but never forget the meaning of the text. It is seldom that we hear a song or an *aria* sung in this way; but often we hear one so indifferently rendered that we receive no impression whatever as to the meaning of the music; on this point we find the separating line between ordinary singers and *artists*.

Pupils must learn to decide for themselves as to how a song or *role* is to be prepared from an *intellectual* as well as a musical standpoint. This is arrived at through mental concentration.

A song expresses certain thoughts to be found in the text. It is necessary for the singer to read the text many times until the finest gradations in the underlying thought become clear; then the text must be recited with simplicity and self-control.

The convincing accent of reality must stand supreme over the situation and must give the rendition light and life and hold the minds of the listeners spell-bound.

After the text is understood, the singer must analyze the music, judge its construction and divide the energy where it belongs so as not to fall short when the greatest climax is demanded. Wrong distribution of voice is a very usual fault amongst inexperienced singers.

Imagination is a great help in rendering text with expression whether in *roles* or songs. To impress your audience with a part that you live in an opera, with costumes and scenery, is much easier than to hold your audience with a song in which the underlying poetic thought must be expressed by sheer interpretation.

We have many singers with beautiful voices who are exceedingly uninteresting because they sing only the melody. They may render it well from a musical standpoint; yet we receive no impression, are often bored and glad when they are through.

At times we hear a singer who by nature is endowed with the sacred spark, but who has had little or no vocal culture, yet he may give his audience far more genuine pleasure than the singer who has culture and no imaginative interpretation.

We have all experienced disappointment at the changes in some voices after study, when the natural voice was far more musical and expressive than the cultured, in this case, of course, wrongly cultured, voice. In many cases the study robs the voice of its fresh tonal beauty and thus indirectly hinders the singer from giving his best.

All good compositions are inspired by the text, therefore first of all get at the deepest understanding of it, and next, render the music as nearly like the composer's ideas as possible. These rules should be adhered to always and the singer will in time find a vast improvement in his development, — the subconscious mind will then work for him. Many a surprise is in store for those who seek knowledge in the right way.

Regarding translations I can only say that often they are bad; but we have good translations and with time they will be better. I think that any text can be translated into English if it falls into the right hands; but many poor translations exist and should be avoided.

For those studying *Lieder*, do not be afraid of Schubert. Even if difficult, Schubert is, after all, the master and much more modern than we think. Then there are Schumann, Franz, Brahms, and, lastly, Hugo Wolf; but the lovely Mozart and Beethoven *Lieder* should not be forgotten. They all cultivate our taste. Do not take an antagonistic attitude towards the classic composers, — the study of them is never lost work.

Opera singers should learn Mozart, Gluck, Meyerbeer and Verdi; there is time later to sing the modern German, French and Italian composers.

It is a great fault to attempt the short road to success in art. If you are a genius, the way is made for you; if not, you must work your way, which takes time, but which alone brings results.

Learn to concentrate your mind upon your undertaking; to avoid the pitfalls of automatic routine and mere mechanical practice. Let the mind assist you in every department of your study and thus develop individuality. Never forget that singing is an intellectual art, as painting and sculpture are intellectual arts.

Poise or Attitude of Body Towards Voice

From explanations given in previous chapters we have learned that the voice, together with the various tone-colors, is dependent upon a normal breath-form; and to enable a proper form of breath, the body must be in a state of ease and in a responsive condition. The trunk of the body should feel comfortable upon the members supporting it and the body attitude (poise) should from the very beginning become second nature. In the first place an easy poise gives freedom to those performing muscles which are taxed during singing, puts the body in perfect harmony and effects comfort in our work.

Never permit the rigid leg to be the rear leg. The rigid leg supports the body and must always be in front of the relaxed leg; a trifle forward suffices, only enough is necessary to prevent the body from resting on both legs at the same time, as this is as ungraceful as it is impracticable. The very bad habit of letting the rigid leg be the rear leg causes the body to fall together, contracts the breath-form and causes other complications which the student who is aspiring to Opera will meet.

For the proper rendition of songs, the correct poise of the body is of great importance, as it produces a most telling effect during expressive moments.

Do not hold the hands as if in prayer neither fill the pockets with them; these are disturbing habits which later on can be overcome only with superhuman control. Observe and criticise yourself before a mirror, taking notice of your facial expression as well as the position of your body. A mirror tells the truth and you can learn much by its aid.

The more we accustom ourselves to natural grace in the beginning, the less we will have to undo later on and the more elastic will become our movements while enacting a *role*.

Concentration

I may say without exaggeration, that no art requires more concentration than that of singing. As the result ceases with the tone, it is all-important that the memory be strengthened. Concentration is a great aid in this direction, while at the same time it gives additional strength to the hearing and feeling. The sooner the student is able to follow the trend of the vocal mind, the surer and quicker will be his development. Every exercise should be sung with full understanding as to the "why." The thoughts should constantly be fastened upon the freedom of tone, on vowel-form and the perfection of intonation. Comfort in the production of the voice must be aimed at, all forcing and "screaming" must be excluded. Every good result achieved must be examined into so that the same result may be repeatedly accomplished and with less effort and more freedom if possible. A proper intonation through correct attack and not only through hearing, which is instrumental in the judgment, must be our aim. Never produce a tone by pushing the intonation high by the heargin, — let the tone intonate automatically through correct production.

Those who in the beginning find singing a pleasure and a pastime while practicing should question themselves from time to time as to whether the well-produced tones are accidental or really the result of training and thinking. Repetitions should never be carried so far as to tire the mind or to impair concentration. Neither is it a proof of good practice that a student has sung all the high notes in his voice. The high voice takes care of itself when the low and medium voices are in good condition and finely produced.

Many times the question is put to me,— "How long should one practise a day?" For the beginner I should suggest three times daily, each time twenty minutes; for advanced students, two hours daily but not all at one time. But conditions alter these rules greatly. For those who are studying a *repertoire*, more time can be given; but the individual should never over-fatigue nor overwork himself, which is worse than devoting too little time to practice.

The result of over-work is generally felt on the following day. A rest of a couple of days to refresh the system is most beneficial. However, care should be exercised not to repeat over-taxing, as a failure invariably follows, if only temporarily.

The surer the singer is of his technique the less need there is for him to "sing in." I have pupils who, *without preparation*, will start early in the morning with the most difficult arias, which is due to proper concentration, the correct tone being first placed in the mind before being rendered. The mind must be prepared for singing and if well prepared it can undertake any task. This condition of preparedness is not easily reached and can only be acquired by one who esteems the value of real mental vocal concentration.

General Review

From all that has preceded we see that the actual mechanical causes of tone production have been analyzed in a simple way.

The word *normal* appears very frequently in our treatise, — normal as regards growth through the eradication of whatever natural deficiencies may be present, including errors so frequently *trained into* voice production. Our knowledge as to cause and effect is to help overcome existing faults and wrong conceptions as to how and where resonance is obtained, produced or placed, and to prevent fancies and misunderstandings regarding breath.

Speaking of *cause* and *effect*, I once more mention that the vocal chords are the definite producers. The perfect control of the vocal chords can be obtained only where no overbalance or pressure of the breath exists. The first and all-important training is to enable the student to hear the difference between a perfect resonating tone and a breathy or diffused tone, and never to let the voice diffuse in *diminuendo*. The tangible way of guiding the adjustment of the form of the vocal tube is through the pure vowels. Standing supreme above all is our *sense of hearing*, which can never be trained too keenly in recognition of the free floating tone with perfect vowel form, perfect intonation and perfect tone-color, expressing the musical as well as the intellectual meaning of the *word* coupled with the *music*.

Further, I wish to state that the art of singing, of which breathing is an integral part, is almost entirely an art *mentally controlled*. The moment the abstract becomes concrete knowledge, the mentality steps into control and demands of the subconscious vocal organs the desired result. Where no unnatural error has been allowed to enter into the training, the physical vocal organs are always obedient, if we do not demand of them that which Nature has not intended, — for instance a barytone to sing tenor or a mezzo to sing dramatic soprano and similar unreasonable demands. In fact, every student should as soon as possible find his classification; the limitations usually take care of themselves when the student enters into the arena of public work, where kind friends no longer have any weight with their generously bestowed compliments.

The individuality of the singer will grow and develop through the development of the mental side of our art.

The physical development must always go hand in hand with the mental side, or our art becomes a test of athletic forcing of mechanical unmusical tones that express nothing but a melody in a tone-volume that leaves the listener perhaps for a moment surprised, but usually unsatisfied and uninterested.

CHAPTER XII
The Low Larynx

The training of a singer to lower the larynx for the production of a certain quality of tone has been successful to some extent, but at the great risk of making the voice darker than normal. The vowel-sound that is most effective in lowering the larynx is *oo*. The position of the *oo* larynx has no value if it is accompanied by a loosening of the inner width of the vocal tube, hence the continued improper use of *oo* involves the danger of making the upper voice thin and "hooting," besides reducing the vibratory brilliance of the vowel-sound *ee*.

However, those who understand the value and right use of the low larynx are at great advantage in their art. The tones between C and G in high medium voice, with low grooved tongue of the syllable *ah*, are only possible of production with a loose, low larynx, and no amount of patience (but not forcing) expended on this point of technique will be wasted time.

The singer whose tongue rises in the back around D, E and F before entering the higher range, has not yet found the free balanced natural scale that ascends into the top range.

In working for the ideal condition of the low larynx, I would prefer calling it a loose, low, open, comfortable throat. We must start with these conditions from our lowest tones. What changes the larynx upward is usually a wrong idea of covering the voice on D, E and F by making the tone more nasal and dark and changing the vowel-sound, for example from *ah* to *aw*, or *oh* toward *oo*, or *ee* toward *a*. These are compromises; and even if at times we hear good artists employing them, we must not accept them. The singer with perfect knowledge of pure vowels in low and medium voice, who ascends without pressing on the breath or placing the tone nasally forward, is able to bring his art to the point of singing all vowels with ease throughout the entire range.

I know very well that these conditions are rare, and that I am contradicted on this point by many teachers and artists. Still my proof remains: the results demonstrated by pupils, and I feel bound to insist that those who are not able to produce all vowels with equal ease throughout their entire range, are still deficient in technical knowledge of their own voices.

The understanding of the so-called low larynx, used without pressure or wrong covering, will enable the singer to attain this ideal condition. But forced breath, wrongly covered tone production and too great an effort at feeling the resonance in one place, are suggestions of danger, and are apt to impair the keener sense of hearing the voice in its natural individual tone-color.

CHAPTER XIII
The Trill

The *trill* or *shake* is a valuable asset to any singer, directly, as an embellishment of the voice; indirectly, as a test of the singer's knowledge of the use of the voice.

We have singers with trills as natural as those of birds; others are less favored, while many appear to be incapable of this beautiful effect.

The trill is produced by the regular oscillation or shaking of the larynx and its chief requisite is *intonation*. Whether the trill is on half or whole tone, it must be generously intonated and the *rhythm* must be regular, preferably fast; too slow a trill has little charm.

When a steady tone is to be converted into a trill, the larynx is allowed to become very loose; instinct will inform the singer to what degree. Three conditions must be observed:

First: the intonation must be perfect. If one of the two tones is too covered, the intonation is lowered and breath pressure ensues;

Second: The larynx must be kept loose, otherwise the breath pressure becomes too tight and the trill too slow;

Third: the vibrations of the vocal chords must not be *over-relaxed*, otherwise the tone becomes diffused, the trill is small and weak and cannot be carried through *crescendo* and *diminuendo*.

Practically the trill is an *automatic* movement of the larynx controlled up to a certain point by the singer, who regulates the approach and duration of the trill; but the speed or rhythm of the movement, once it begins, becomes independent of conscious control. This is true, of course, only in the case of a perfect trill, which is produced without effort.

When the attempt is wrongly started through imperfect comprehension of forward placing, the voice simply refuses to produce the shake. In such cases the apparently radical remedy of keeping the trill broad against the back wall of the throat will release the constriction and the shake will appear.

But general suggestions and advice relating to the trill are difficult to give. The teacher should have each voice under observation before he can determine what special remedies to apply to special faults.

The trill is possible of achievement by any singer, but where it has never been produced or has been lost, the teacher must get a complete conception of the particular voice and apply the logic suitable to the case.

As a Remedy for Tremolo

The study of the trill has, in my experience, proved a remedy for the *tremolo* where all else has failed.

The alternation from sustained tones to trills in the middle voice has brought out the contrast in the production of these two tones, and through the *sensing* of the difference in connection with the *hearing*, the singer has been enabled to control an otherwise tremulous voice.

But this operation must be guided by one who thoroughly understands the subject.

Staccato

The first time I heard Adelina Patti sing, I sat in the last row of the gallery, and the *diva* on the stage looked so remote and small I thought I should not hear her when she sang. It was music that seemed to come from a different world, so wonderful it was and so simple; but I shall never forget her first *staccato* notes. The bell-like tone, with its peculiar carrying power, was so intense that I, with several others, looked about to see if some one nearer to us was singing. This illustrates how the *staccato* of the human voice, in regard to balance and carrying power, represents the minimum effort and the maximum result.

The *staccato* is found more frequently among the high female voices, but can be produced in any voice; naturally, in the male voice it will assume a different quality.

The first essential preparatory condition in producing *staccato* is perfectly free breath-form. Lilli Lehmann, in her later years, terms this "the staccato breath-form." In the production of perfect *staccato*, the cause and effect become interchangeable, so to speak. The moment the breath-form becomes too intense, the vocal chords automatically resist the unnecessary pressure and thus the wonderful quality of balance is lost.

The second essential of the *staccato* is that the tone shall not be *placed*. Some singers form a mental picture of the tone, which might conceivably be of assistance in individual cases; but I advise against placing it anywhere, as it is apt to become pointed and thus the floating quality is lost.

I know of no branch of singing that has greater fascination and is better training for the sense of hearing than the study of *staccato*.

It is also of great use to singers who have no definite *pianissimo*. Repeat several *staccatos*, say four, then sustain the fifth without changing breath-form or *gripping* the tone or darkening it, and without increasing the volume. This exercise will be found very useful in achieving good *pianissimo*, and will aid the singer to realize the full resources of the voice and thus establish a more independent feeling.

Bad Methods

There is a *staccato* widely used by German singers, which is produced more like a flute tone and sounds like the vowel-sound "*oo*." This is effected by a diffused voice, badly closed vocal chords and, if used to any great extent, is a detriment to the vocal organs. The damaging results are first shown in loss of brilliancy in the top voice, lack of *crescendo* on B♭ and higher; but most detrimental of all is the definite tendency to get-off key immediately after its use, as well as a tendency to huskiness.

The reason for these effects is that the vocal chords are not in normal adjustment and use, and a consequent confusion ensues between the physical and mental control. These tones sound at times like those of a ventriloquist and I cannot advise too strongly against this method of producing *staccato*.

In the female voice inability to produce *staccato* usually is due to unnatural pressure against the larynx and the consequent displacement of the vocal organs. Under such conditions the singer is unable to produce the wonderful bell-like resonance that characterizes true *staccato*.

CHAPTER XIV

Song and Songs

Song was given to us to express many of the deepest emotions of life. Joy, sorrow, love, religious fervor, patriotism, find what is perhaps the most adequate expression in song. The music of song is an international language and we all have experienced the inspiring effect of melody wherever it originated; but the deepest meaning of song is never wholly felt until we have words of beauty and grace wedded to music that fully interprets them and sung by one whose mind and heart unite with the voice to send forth a message almost divine.

But the truth is that such inspirational quality of song is too often lost in the singer's eagerness for display and loud applause. Such a singer leaves the judicious hearer empty and discouraged.

Songs are written for that type of performer and a long-sustained high tone on the syllable "ah" invariably captures an audience, while an intelligent and sympathetic interpretation of a song made of really beautiful words and music, will arouse but languid interest.

Thus we have a large body of mediocre song material thrust upon us by mediocre writers and singers. If our current book literature was of as low a standard as much of the prevailing music, it would be destroyed as poisonous to the mind.

I therefore ask my fellow-teachers to do all in their power to bring only the best of songs to the hearing of their pupils. The meretricious, half-stolen product of inferior writers that appeals only to the barren mind, must be left to perish of neglect. The classics will never die and good modern songs are being written, worthy of the greatest singers; but taste in music has fallen to a low condition among the multitude, and we who profess to bring understanding of song to the young mind, must regard ourselves as apostles of song in its highest estate, and only those who devote themselves to its advancement have the right to teach.

Study of the old masters is as essential in the education of the singer as it is in the pursuit of the companion arts of painting and sculpture; and it is only by such study and training that the student is enabled readily to distinguish between good and bad examples of modern work.

A great movement, collateral to the work of the vocal teacher, is in progress throughout our public schools and demands the support of every true citizen. By the use of good songs in our schools the young mind is reached at a period of life when impressions are most easily made and retained; and it must not be forgotten that the impressions of poor music are as easily made and last quite as long. It is the duty of the vocal teacher whose pupil has had the advantage of sound school training in good musical taste, to continue the work begun in school and by every means in his power to encourage its wholesome growth; to "take up the torch and never let it fall."

The Mental Side of Singing

In other parts of this book the mental and physical features of singing have been treated sometimes separately and at other times together; it is difficult to dissociate them, as they are so closely interrelated.

But the mental side requires special mention since, in the final analysis the perfect art of singing chiefly depends on *mental control*.

It is, of course, the teacher's duty to discover and seek to correct physical errors that impede the development of the pupil's chosen art; but as we approach normal tone-production from the physical point of view, great attention should be given to the mental influence over all phases of singing.

We must teach imagination; the singer must be brought to realize and understand that singing means thoughts expressed in words and melody, and that to express fully and deeply, we must *feel* fully and deeply; that the better we comprehend and exercise the function of the mind as the controlling influence over all physical manifestations, the more beautiful the voice becomes and the more certainly it will take on the tone-colors the mind desires to express.

This indispensible mental condition is impossible where an unnatural technique has been imposed on the student instead of the principles of fundamental simplicity which underlie the true art of singing.

Unfortunate is the student who, after years of study, is still seeking what he has been taught to call "the placement of the voice." How much better it would be for everybody concerned if the term "voice placement" could be abolished and the student simply *learn to sing!*

Where instruction has been dissociated from Nature and wrong principles forced on the pupil, little but confusion results. The mental side is being opposed continually by the physical which is being wrongly trained and cannot respond to the mental impulse.

The most reliable and successful artists are and always have been the ones who have developed their art on natural, simple and therefore correct lines and have added to physical perfection of tone an intelligent comprehension of the function of mental control. Given a physical training hand in hand with Nature, and the mind will control your breath, your tone-colors; it will enter the realms of imagination and select for you the forms and lines of expression and guide you in imparting them faithfully to your audience.

Balance

The word *balance* is frequently found throughout this work, and perhaps needs a definite explanation. Tone production is a result of certain physical actions and reactions, chief among which are the vibratory qualities, produced by the vocal chords, and the resonances or results of vibratory action, produced in the head. These are described in other chapters. *Balance*, as a factor in perfect singing, is of equal if not greater importance. We use the terms over- and under-balance in our explanations of various effects, meaning thereby a tendency either to press or over-relax; but the real significance of *balance* lies deeper than that. It includes *everything* that has to do with singing; the mental side of the art as affected by the senses of hearing and of feeling, correlated with the physical reactions, all under control of the *Mind*, which must be trained to perfect mastery of the situation. Thus perfect balance is attained, without which perfect singing is impossible.

This perfection is rarely found. The many contradictory modern ideas about so-called "tone-placing" have so confused the minds of our singers that the ideal of perfection is seldom achieved. This ideal could more nearly be approached if a greater degree of common sense and fewer fads were employed by some of the teaching fraternity, and if only those of real talent and voice would attempt the profession of singing.

CHAPTER XV
The Hygiene of the Voice
Colds

The familiar bugbear of singers is the "cold," and the theory is held by some that a singer's cold is somehow different from other colds.

This is not true except in the sense that a cold interferes more directly with the singer's vocation than in the case of a layman similarly afflicted.

We often hear the expression, "singing over a cold." There is no such thing. We sing with a cold as we do without it, and some artists, by the practice of the true principles of singing, are able to overcome in a measure, the handicap of a cold. But my experience leads me to warn against the use of the voice under such conditions. The singer with a cold should be treated like anybody else with a cold, and the greatest safety for the voice lies in not using it at such times.

The Throat

The singer's throat, if used naturally, should be at least as healthy and responsive as other throats. If it is not, the reason, in ninety-nine cases in a hundred, is that the throat is being abused in some one or more of the many ways of abusing a throat. If the wrong use of the throat always resulted in an immediate inability to sing at all, it would be a blessing to the singer; but there are so many subtle degrees of wrong use and consequent impairment of the throat and so many compromises available, that the sufferer frequently deceives himself into a belief that excuses error.

The singer who has no voice in the early hours of the day would do well to investigate the cause. There is no reason why we should not find our first tones free and clear in the early morning, unless the vocal organs have been recently misused; and in this connection it must be noted that loud and nasal talking is as bad for the voice as wrong singing.

Causes of Trouble

Bad digestion, derangement of liver, physical reaction from over-indulgence in food and drink, late hours, etc., are prime causes of the impairment of natural energy and brilliance of the voice. A singer should lead a simple, healthy and natural life, if the voice is to be kept simple, healthy and natural.

With regard to smoking — some do and some do not. Many a singer smokes and still keeps his voice in a fairly reliable condition. My advice is against smoking, especially against inhalation of the smoke. On the whole, I believe the practice will eventually get the better of the voice.

Fear

Fear, usually taking the form of nervousness at the beginning of a performance and often called "stage fright," resulting in hoarseness and uncertainty, should be eliminated from the singer's consciousness.

This is easier to say than to accomplish. In too many cases the singer has very good reasons for fear, due to lack of confidence inseparable from bad teaching and erroneous practice.

The correct correlation between the mental and physical attributes of song will insensibly lead the singer into logical channels of interpretation. The sense of *control* that comes with the feeling that the voice is being used correctly, develops courage and authority, and fear vanishes. The mind takes charge, so to speak, and tone-color responds to mental command; the singer *lives* the song and the individual is lost in the artist.

The Teacher's Function

Obviously the teacher is largely involved in the process of converting *fear* into *courage*. The pupil does not reach the ideal we have pictured without important help by the teacher. And the factor of mental suggestion by the latter, the changing of a wrong mental picture or attitude by the suggestion of the true, logical and natural picture or attitude, is invaluable in this behalf. My experience has shown me that as soon as the mental attitude coincides with the thought to be expressed, the voice becomes obedient and interpretative and the confidence of the singer is increased accordingly.

Hoarseness

We often find students hoarse after singing whose voices were clear before. This is positive proof that such voices have been improperly used. We find the condition oftener among men singers, but the female voice does not escape. Forcing and pressing will cause hoarseness as well as singing with diffused and breathy tone. Whatever the cause, the singer who suffers from hoarseness after singing should take instant warning that something is wrong and take measures to correct it. A voice continuously abused, even in small degree, will soon lose that indefinable charm of freshness, and unfortunately that loss will often be noted by the listener before it is realized by the singer.

Another condition that requires notice is hoarseness in

one register while the other remains clear. Sometimes this is due to a slight cold, but more frequently it is the result of overtaxing the voice. It takes the form of partial congestion of the vocal chords. If it occurs in the back of the larynx, the low voice is affected; if in the front, the high voice becomes husky. In either case, *do not sing*, if singing can be avoided.

It may be well to state that the low-voice huskiness is less dangerous than the other.

General Advice

After a winter spent in artificial heat, be careful how you talk and sing. With the first spring days we are apt to "rush the season" and the well-known "spring cold" develops. The ancient advice to singers: "Keep the mouth closed when not singing" is good today. It means nothing more than to be careful not to waste the voice or use it unnecessarily or carelessly.

Advice as to bathing the face, neck and chest is good advice; but the practice will not insure the singer against indisposition due to careless dressing and living. As we have said before, the **singer, of all people, must live a healthy and normal life.**

CHAPTER XVI

Suggestions in Plastic

This chapter is written for both the concert and the opera aspirant.

The term *plastic* is here used as a convenient one to indicate the art of expression by means of gesture, attitude, poise, direction of the eyes, and by other appropriate movements. A knowledge of plastic is most valuable to all who wish to master the art of expression. The accompanying *Tables of Poise and Gesture* will repay careful study and be of great assistance to the student.

Concert Singers

A few general hints may be of use to the singer of songs.

Do not hold the hands in an attitude of prayer. Learn that the hands, as well as other members and features of the body, are capable of a wonderful variety of expression (see *Tables*) which will be lost if they are used aimlessly.

Do not move the body or any member without knowing clearly why you do so and for the purpose of aiding your interpretation. The smallest gradation of attitude or gesture, if co-ordinated with the thought to be expressed, will, in a natural and unaffected way, strengthen your effect and give you authority and ease.

If your song has a prelude, use this as a means of establishing your physical as well as mental attitude toward the song. And it is important to remember to keep your final facial expression and physical poise for a moment after your song has ceased or until the end of the afterlude, if any is played.

Analysis of a song and practice in physical interpretation before the mirror will be found extremely useful.

Unexpectedly favorable results will follow study along these lines. Dr. Willmer, to my mind the greatest interpreter of songs of this age, in singing Schubert's *Erl King*, for example, could express every mood of that wonderful song by movements of his hands or fingers and the position of his head, though he seemed to be almost motionless; the least change in his poise meant something and he utilized every resource of physical expression with the minimum of effort and the result was magnificent.

Opera

To the student of opera my first advice is to obtain the fullest and deepest understanding of the character to be portrayed. If it is a classic part, study the illustrations of the character; then visualize your audience; classify the emotions you are to express; study the corresponding expressions on the *Tables* and practice them before the mirror. You will soon feel that what you are seeking to express is taking physical form in accordance with your mental conception. Correct your mistakes as they occur. Study the head positions and the arm gestures, taking care that the latter are within the general field of Soul, Heart, Life.

Remember that the fewer the gestures, the more effective they will be; but though few, make them powerful and full of meaning. Practice freedom of gesture and poise and observe the simple rule of arm movements in relation to the weight of the body, i.e. the gesture of the right arm should be accompanied by relaxation of the right leg, and *vice versa*. Make your gesture slightly in advance of the corresponding utterance, and hold it appreciably after the voice has ceased.

But study must be assisted by actual experience in operatic work before anything real is achieved. Traditions are to be learned and innumerable refinements absorbed that cannot be imparted by study alone. My purpose in touching this subject is merely to give the student certain lines of thought and certain elementary rules and warnings.

CHAPTER XVII
Tables of Poise and Gesture
HEAD

VENERATION	Right	Down
REFLECTION	Straight	Down
SUSPICION	Left	Down
TENDERNESS	Right	Recline
COLOURLESS	Straight	
PLEASURE	Left	Recline
ABANDONMENT	Right	Recline
EXHALTATION	Straight	Recline
PRIDE	Left	Recline

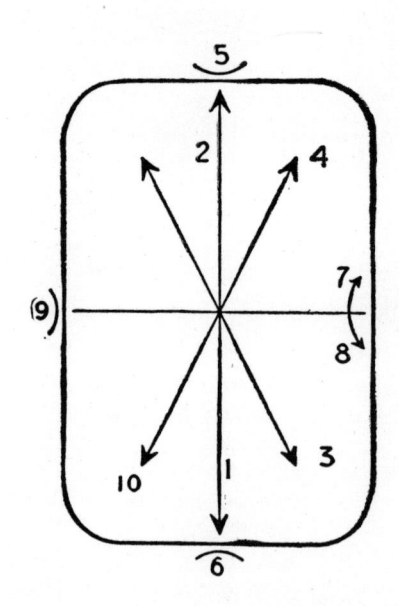

ARM GESTURES

SOUL: From shoulder vertically upward
HEART: From shoulder vertically straight
LIFE: From shoulder vertically down

DIRECTION OF GESTURES

(See chart on opposite page)

1. TOP TO BOTTOM   Affirmation
2. BOTTOM UPWARD   Hope
3. TOP TO BOTTOM   Rejection
4. BOTTOM UPWARD   Disdain
5. PALMS UPWARD   Quietude
6. PALMS DOWN   Secret
7. BOTTOM UPWARD   Moral delicacy
8. TOP TO BOTTOM   Physical delicacy

POISE

The arm over relaxed leg should execute gesture, never the arm over stiff leg. Stiff leg always in any pose to be a trifle forward.

EYES

DESCRIPTIVE TERMS

CONCENTRO: Relaxed; drawn together
EXCENTRO: Expanded; open
NORMAL

	EYEBROWS	EYES
REFLECTION	Concentro	Concentro
EXHAUSTION	Normal	Concentro
DISDAIN	Excentro	Concentro
BAD HUMOR	Concentro	Normal
COLOURLESS	Normal	Normal
INDIFFERENCE	Excentro	Normal
FIRMNESS	Concentro	Excentro
STUPOR	Normal	Excentro
SURPRISE	Excentro	Excentro

	Hands	Fingers
Struggle	Concentro	Concentro
Power–Authority	Normal	Thumb over
Convulsive	Excentro	Finger tips bent
Prostration	Normal	Normal
Abandonment	Normal	Thumb under
Expansion	Normal	Excentro thumb out
Hatred	Concentro	Last joints bend in
Exhaltation	Normal	Hands open
Exasperation	Excentro	Fingers slightly bent
The Back of Your Hand		Mystic
Palm of Your Hand		Picture
Tips of Your Fingers		Teaching

EXERCISES

The dotted lines under the vowels are to assist the student to visualize the convex and concave tongue-positions for bright, neutral and dark vowels.

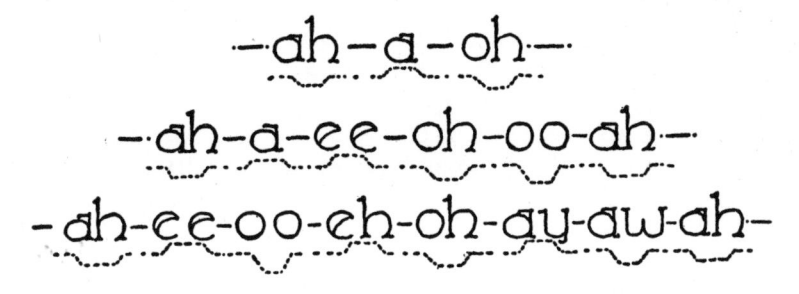

—ah—a—oh—

—ah—a—ee—oh—oo—ah—

—ah—ee—oo—eh—oh—ay—aw—ah—

Exercise 1

ah . . . . a . . . . oh . . . . .

This exercise brings the voice in both directions from the initial tone, one whole step upward, one-half step downward. Care should be taken that the resonance does not change after the voice moves upward from the first tone. The *bite*, the *ping*, the clearness of the resonance, must not diminish, neither must the definite form of the vowel change. If the brilliance or resonance of the voice becomes dull, breath is wasted, the vocal chords do not close perfectly. Therefore in order that we may start our first exercise as nearly perfect as possible, articulate with clear normal full voice the words *day; go; art*. Hear and feel the point of articulation where the vowel is produced, and then sing — hesitating an instant between inhalation and articulation of the first vowel in the exercise. Stand erect but relaxed, and take the pitch from the piano; use great care to get perfect intonation; do not forget to inhale slowly through nose with lips slightly apart, and let the tip of tongue rest gently against lower teeth, with bright but not exaggerated inner smile. After having sung the exercise **one or** more times in the same key, progress upward and downward, as far as can be done comfortably, not going so high that the voice gets thin or breathy, nor so low that the tone in female voices becomes chesty, or masculine. Some voices have at first greater facility starting with *ah*, others with *a* or *oh*. This is dependent upon the condition of the voice. A voice with tendency to breathiness should start with the vowel *a* — taking care that it is not nasal. This can be tested by pinching the nostrils while singing. Voices that are too white or blatant can to advantage start with *oh*. Under normal conditions I prefer starting with the vowel *ah* as in the wort *art.*

Exercise 2

ah . . a . . ee . . oh . . oo . . ah . . .

Follow the same procedure as in No. 1, but use six vowel sounds, starting with *ah* (concave tongue very important); then *a* and *ee* (convexed or arched tongue); then *oh* and *oo* (again concave and still lower root of tongue or larynx). Take care that *oo* does not sound dull, but do not press it forward against the teeth, which is very detrimental. If it is not possible to produce *oo* clearly at first, a few days practice usually places this vowel correctly, especially if we do not try too hard; and the last *ah* must be as brilliant as the first *ah*. The repetition of this exercise, since it is twice the length of No. 1, naturally takes more breath; but this regulates itself after a few repetitions, as we learn instinctively to inhale the amount of breath we need. Do not forget the gentle inner smile on all vowels, as that regulates the palate in keeping certain vowels from becoming nasal in contrast to others. This is of the utmost importance in training the sense of hearing and feeling in unison.

Exercise 3

[musical notation]

ah . . . ee . . . oo . . . eh . . .

oh . . . ay . . . aw . . . ah . . . .

Procedure is the same as Nos. 1 and 2; but we sing on eight vowel sounds, starting with the neutral vowel *ah* and proceed with alternating concave and convex vowel, or tongue positions; in other words *bright* and *dark* vowels. This training is all important and its aim in this exercise is to produce the changes of different vowels. It should be accomplished without discomfort. Do not change the outer mouth too much. It is mostly a training of inner mouth vowel production, not an exercise in phonetics.

Exercise 4

[musical notation]

ah . . . . a . . . . oh . . . . . .

Scales of four tones are very important; the fourth interval must be intonated perfectly. The choice of vowels for this exercise depends upon the condition of voice, but *ah, a* and *oh* are best under normal conditions. For high voices this exercise can be sung between C and G, progression by half tones; low voices from A to E. Do not forget to breathe rather slowly and comfortably relaxed. *Think* the exercise while you inhale. In this way you train normal breathing under absolute instinctive mental control.

Exercise 5

[musical notation]

ah . . . . . . a . . . . . . ee . . . . .
oh . . . . . oo . . . . . ah . . . . .

The same as No. 3 but with six vowels sounds, and consequently a deeper breath.

Exercise 6

[musical notation]

ah . . . . . . a . . . . . oh . . . .

Scale of five tones, each scale on the vowel sounds *ah, a, oh*. It is important to take the fuller breath for the first scale and then a catch breath or half breath between scales; progressing by half tones, a deeper breath before each new key. This is the first exercise where we call the attention to *full* and *half* breath; later this exercise can be sung with ease and comfort in one breath on all vowels. Usually it is not necessary to think about the catch breath; instinct regulates it for us. I mention it to show the purpose of the exercise.

Exercise 7

[musical notation]

ah . . . a . . . oh . . . .

Sing the scale upward without any pressure of the breath, **or** pinching or effort, and if the scale is perfectly produced, the pupil will experience no trouble in discontinuing the tone; but it must be finished without diminishing, gracefully and without effort. The detachment of the top tone of the scale prepares for the start of the following one. This exercise is most important at this stage, in order that we may not overburden the vocal organs with pressure in the attack or discontinuance of the tone.

Exercise 8

ah . . . . oh . . . . a . . . .

The same as No. 7, except that we attack on top tone of scale. Great care must be taken in No. 8 that the descending scales terminate thin and clear without any burden. Under no circumstances should beginners sing Nos. 7 and 8 above G for high voices or E flat for lower voices.

Exercise 9

ah . . . . a . . . . .

. . . . oh . . . .

This a combination of No. 1 and No. 6. Can be sung separately on each vowel sound like No. 6, or all in one breath, and same vowels as under normal conditions *ah, a, oh*.

Exercise 10

a . . . . oh . . . . oh . . . ah . . .

The purpose of this exercise is to equalize high and low tone color; take care of the breathform; do not lift on the high scale; try to match the tone-color so that the ear is pleased and the throat comfortable.

Exercise 11

The same as No. 10; but more deeply relaxed breathing is necessary to keep the same tone-color in upper and lower scale. Neither No. 10 nor 11 need be sung above G for high voices, and about E or F for the lower voices.

Exercise 12

The scale of eight vowel sounds on seven tones is a most important exercise. The progression of the voice rather slowly, changing vowels on each tone and intonating the fourth and seventh intervals are important factors in vocal technique; also this is our first step in the technique of sustained work.

Exercise 13

This scale is the first step toward producing the voice smaller in size than normal. The *staccato* is the minimum attack possible for the voice, if properly executed. The first four *staccato* notes produced as short and bell-like as possible, give us the position of the *pianissimo* and we continue our scale on the fifth *staccato*, which turns into the first tone of the scale. The breath-form created through the *staccato* is the breath-form for *pianissimo* and the normal vowels *ah, a, oh* should be kept in the same place from the standpoint of sensing; the tone-color will then automatically equalize itself. This exercise should not be sung with too much voice.

Exercise 14

ah . . . .

This exercise is of benefit for agility and top voice. Should mostly be used by female voices, care to be taken not to sing the the *staccatos* heavily. A slight *crescendo* towards the top of upper scale is advantageous, but be careful not to induce the sensation of leaning against any one place; keep the tone free and floating; guard against the hard quality that comes from forcing.

Exercise 15

ah ah ah ah ah ah ah ah ah . . . .

ah . . . .

This exercise is for the female voice. The scale of nine *staccato* notes must be clear as a bell — the descending scale no heavier than the *staccato*, and the second scale upward with gradual *crescendo*. This is a most important scale for the uniting of smaller and heavier volume on the same breath. The exercise must not lose the quality of the *staccato* throughout its duration.

Exercise 16

(musical notation with "a .... oh ...." and "ah ....")

The scale of five and nine tones with *a, oh, ah*, is very simple. Care should be taken that the scales of five tones are never sung heavy, and with only a gradual crescendo towards the end of the scale of nine tones. This exercise is beneficial for all voices and can be sung within the range of any voice from lowest to highest; but always guard against pressing on the last tone of scale. Too much attention cannot be given on this point.

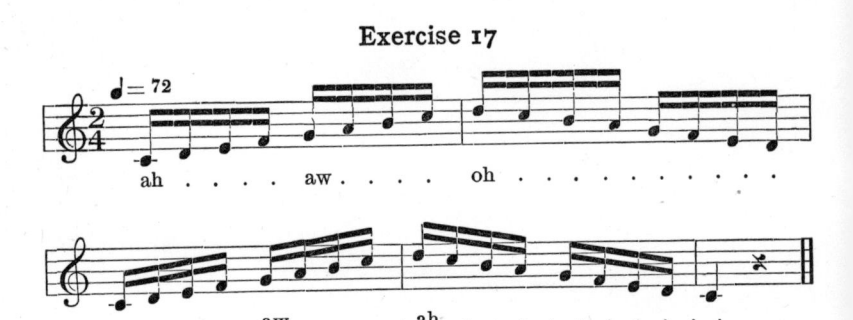

Exercise 17

(musical notation with "ah ... aw ... oh ...." and "... aw ... ah ....")

This scale of twice nine tones with the alternating of dark and neutral vowel sounds *oh* and *ah* at top and bottom of scale, is to train the pupil in discerning a *crescendo*, not dependent on darkening of the voice. The first ascending scale from *ah, aw* to *oh*, must not darken, and the following scale from *oh, aw* to *ah* must not become white or blatant. This is a most practical exercise for any voice and is excellent training in tone color and vowel form.

Exercise 18

ah . . . .

ah . . . .

This scale of nine tones skipping is to train equality of tone-color and is to be sung in the same manner as Nos. 10 and 11, except that greater care should be taken that the upper scale is sung without the breath pressing upward. This warning is especially for those who have been used to draw in the abdomen while singing.

Exercise 19

ah   ee   oh   oo   ah   ah   ee   o   oo   ah

a   ee   o   oo   ah   a   ee   oh   oo   ah

The slow scale has always been a stumbling block for most singers — this because it is almost impossible for any voice to begin sustained singing without the preliminary understanding of a certain amount of relaxed flexibility. This means freedom of larynx. The student must realize that a stiff, fixed larynx or throat position makes it almost impossible to ascend gracefully and slowly with changing vowel sounds. This difficult exercise of changing vowels on the slow scale is of great benefit once mastered, and is the key to all beautiful *legato* and sustained singing. Great patience is needed here at first, but perseverance and severe self-criticism will be well rewarded. Watch intonation.

Exercise 20

a . . . . oh . . . ah . . . .

The turn in scale of five tones descending with gradual *crescendo* is of greatest benefit to low voice but can be used to advantage with all voices. Care must be taken that the lower part of the scale is not produced thick, but on the contrary, full and brilliant without darkening.

Exercise 21

Two octaves in one breath from *pianissimo* to *forte* is a test of technical knowledge and manipulation of breath as well as of tone color. I do not advise the attempt at this exercise too soon, but it is equally beneficial for the voice of both sexes.

Exercise 22

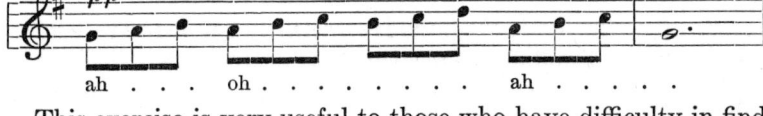

(musical notation: a ... oh ... ah ...)

(musical notation: ah ... oh ... ah ...)

This exercise is very useful to those who have difficulty in finding the legitimate *pianissimo*. For high voice start as low as the voice will respond, even as low as F or G, — sing the low exercise as clearly in *pianissimo* as the low range permits, but always *pianissimo*. Then repeat one octave higher with no more voice but clearer, and take care that the sensing of the tone does not change. This, if done with judgment, is a great help in establishing a perfect reliable *pianissimo*, not diffused and never falsetto.

Exercise 23

(musical notation: a ... oh ... ah ...)

This exercise is for the purpose of searching higher notes in *forte*. The exercise should be started *pianissimo* and increased in volume, descending with a graceful swing. Repeat the upward progression without too much time being devoted to breath.

Exercise 24

(musical notation: ah ... ee .... oo ... eh ...)

(musical notation: oh ... a ... aw ... ah ...)

This entire exercise to be sung *pianissimo* in one breath, but not too fast. A great help in making direct *pianissimo* preparation for text.

Exercise 25

ah aw oh . . aw ah . .   a eh ee . . . eh a . . .

Only where the ear of the pupil is sufficiently trained to recognize pure vowels and undiffused resonance, is it advisable to sing this exercise; but a great opportunity is here offered the student to show ability in perfect singing. If technical errors exist — this exercise will soon disclose them — the test should consist of singing this exercise in the ten succeeding chromatic keys from E flat to C inclusive, without taking the pitch from the piano in any case and to finish intonated.

Exercise 26

The chromatic scale demands the keenest hearing and should be sung sustained, but only where the judgment of the student is very keen as to change of tone color, quiet inhaling and most perfect intonation; great care must be exercised that the last tone in interval is in perfect quality and not short in breath. It must be remembered that the second and the last of the three chromatic scales naturally require a deeper and more plentiful breath than the first scale.

Exercise 27. (The Trill) I

It is well to read the chapter on THE TRILL before attempting the exercises. The first exercise for *staccato* must be sung rather fast, and observe that no upward breath pressure is desired. The trill must start no bigger in volume than *staccato* and the suggestion of loosely lowering the throat while the abdomen relaxes, will quietly help in starting the movement of the trill. Proceed in the next key without hesitancy, and take a small breath at each change of key. This first exercise is to promote facility in the trill but nothing further.

Exercise 28. II

The second exercise is for increasing the rapidity in the trill. It is well to *crescendo* and *diminuendo* one or several times on the sustained trill. All singing based on the *staccato* attack takes less breath, so there is apt to be a surprise in store for those who are not used to sustaining notes with alternate *crescendo* and *diminuendo*.

Exercise 29.   III

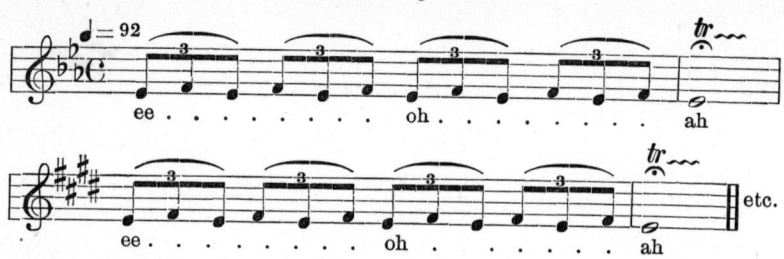

[musical notation: ee ... oh ... ah (with trill); second line similarly ee ... oh ... ah]

The third exercise is for the training of perfect intervals in the trill. The four triplets following each other give the high and low extremes of interval and accent; the vowel *ee* closes the chords and make them thin and flexible; the vowel *oh* lowers the larynx, and the trill on *ah* combines these two qualities in one. The trill has the best opportunity here of being perfect.

Exercise 30.   IV

[musical notation: ah ... ee ... ah ... ee ... ah (with trill); second line similarly]

To the fourth exercise I attach no special importance. I have used it with success in voices that were stiff and stubborn, the principle being this: that in pronouncing *ee* and *ah* in combination with intervals of a third, the larynx is put into similar motion to that of the trill, and if the interval is sung sufficiently fast, it frequently enables the student to terminate on a trill; but this exercise has no importance except in cases of very stubborn nature.

The range in which trills should be attempted is dependent upon the conditions and natural voice tendencies, but always I let my pupils go into the high voice so long as the voice responds to the trill. In some cases the range of the voice where trills can be sustained is very surprising.

The first three exercises, however, are very beneficial in the development of the trill. It must be remembered that the practicing of the trill is healthful study and one of the best exercises to counteract the tendency of heavy singing, for which so much of our modern music is responsible.

Those who seriously study these exercises will notice that the features of flexibility, change of vowel sounds, range, sustained voice, *forte, crescendo* and *diminuendo*, as well as intervals and *pianissimo*, are all, to a considerable extent, covered by these studies. Those desiring further development should consult Manual Garcia's Art of Singing, where the best exercises from the old Italian school are to be found.

For consonant work, I advise simple sustained exercises on single tones according to description in the chapter on Vowels and Consonants. The following table is recommended, care to be taken that the vowel resonance does not become nasal, and that the consonant resonance is not held longer than necessary.

(Consonant Exercise.) *Pah, Bah, Tah, Dah, Kah, Gah, Scha, Djah, Fah, Vah, Sah, Zah, La, Na, Ma, Ra, Gna.*

Other vowels may be substituted with any combination of consonants. I deem this practical for instance; *Bah, Ba, Bee, Boh, Boo*, or other combinations, as long as we abide by the principle of giving each vowel and each consonant its proper resonance as nature has intended: vowels, head resonance, and consonants, mostly nasal resonance.

Finally let me remind the student again to form the habit of articulating the vowel sounds with tip of tongue gently leaning against lower front teeth, and of breathing through a relaxed movement from small of the back downward and sideward without raising chest directly, only as the lungs are gradually filling. These natural principles form a sound, healthy fundamental knowledge, and technique will begin to be established from the first.

It is not to be understood that these exercises are the only ones that can produce results. Any good exercise used with intelligence will produce good results. These have been demonstrated to be practical in cultivating the voice through hearing, the most important factor in singing, after the voice itself.